RICHARD BERG is a Holy Cross priest and the Dean of the College of Arts and Sciences at the University of Portland. His doctor's degree is in psychology with research background in learning and brain physiology. For the past five years he has given retreats on inner healing and served as a spiritual director for priests and laypersons.

CHRISTINE McCARTNEY is presently in the doctoral program in clinical psychology at Purdue University. She holds two master's degrees from the University of Portland in education and criminal justice. During her years as a Christian counselor she has developed a keen sense of the need for understanding depression in terms of the Christian life.

DEPRESSION AND THE INTEGRATED LIFE

DEPRESSION AND THE INTEGRATED LIFE

A Christian Understanding of Sadness and Inner Suffering

Richard F. Berg, C.S.C.

Christine McCartney

ALBA · HOUSE   NEW · YORK

SOCIETY OF ST. PAUL, 2187 VICTORY BLVD., STATEN ISLAND, NEW YORK 10314

Library of Congress Cataloging in Publication Data

Berg, Richard F.
  Depression and the integrated life.

  Includes bibliographical references.
  1. Depression, Mental. I. McCartney, Christine.
II. Title.
RC537.B467   616.85'27   81-7976
ISBN 0-8189-0412-7   AACR2

Designed, printed and bound in the United States of
America by the Fathers and Brothers of the
Society of St. Paul, 2187 Victory Boulevard,
Staten Island, New York 10314, as part of their
communications apostolate.

4 5 6 7 8 9 (Current Printing: first digit).

DEDICATION

With gratitude to Betsy and James Twohy
for their helpful encouragement and wisdom.

FOREWORD

And when He had passed out of the city
He saw seated by the roadside a young
man who was weeping.
And He went forward and touched the long
locks of his hair and said to him,
"Why are you weeping?"
And the young man looked up and recognized
Him and made answer, "But I was dead once
and you raised me from the dead.
What else should I do but weep?"[1]

There are times in our lives when we can sympathize with the young man in the above parable, moments when our living is sad and bitter and depressed. Situations assail us when our existence involves so many conflicts or disappointments that we begin to think in terms of *knots*—that our lives are so inextricably tied up, complicated and confused, that we have lost all sense of smoothness, all lucidity regarding the meaning of what we are doing and where we are going. We can sympathize with the young man because in these moments, these situations, death seems like peace and life is not. All we want to do is cry.

No one is exempt from the above thoughts and feelings. Each of us can identify sources of conflict and disappointment, sources of depression, that can knot up our lives in ways that prohibit peace of mind. This book is about these sources of depression. And it is called, appropriately enough, *Depression and The Integrated Life*. For depression can lead to lack of integration, a *disintegration* in life such that the individual indeed loses his sense of smoothness, his clear awareness of the value or truth of what he is doing and where he is going—in short, his sense of personal worth. He becomes the prey of thoughts and feelings that alienate him from himself and frequently from others.

The excellence of this book, however, derives not only from the sensitivity with which it identifies the sources of depression in our lives (psychological *and* physiological) but also its suggestions for living with and healing depression. Of additional merit is its specific recognition that the religious consciousness of an individual should not be ignored as a ''tool'' for analyzing and healing depression—a recognition that is often absent in other discussions and tends to truncate their helpfulness. I would also note that the book displays a marvelous accessibility to a wide range of readers. It is a worthy exercise not only for the depressed person but for those who live with or counsel depressed people, or just generally for those interested in the phenomenon of depression.

The experience of depression can be little more than an annoyance: it causes only a slight discomfort in our minds and hearts. But it can also be harrowing and destructive—for some people destructive of all sense of purpose in life, destructive even of life itself. Yet for myself I would say that no matter how serious the experience of depression may be, no matter how annoying or destructive, I was continually reminded while reading this book of a place in the gospels that might give any depressed person consolation and strength—the place where it speaks of Jesus feeding the five thousand. For this book has persuaded me that beyond all the depression-producing experiences that may shape our lives we may still have confidence, a confidence in the miraculous that allows something to remain from these experiences beyond our anticipations—something not unlike the bread and fish, the food that remained after feeding the five thousand. Or perhaps better, more exactly said: What remains is the self-knowledge that we must all nourish on experiences that both integrate and disintegrate the meaning we wish our lives to possess.

Jeffrey G. Sobosan
University of Portland
Portland, Oregon

1. Oscar Wilde, *The Poetical Works of Oscar Wilde* (New York: Thomas Y. Crowell Co., 1913), "The Doer of Good," p. 299.

CONTENTS

A Christian Understanding of Sadness and Inner Suffering

INTRODUCTION

It has been called the ``common cold of the mind.'' Mental health authorities conservatively estimate that one in every ten Americans suffers from this energy-sapping, joy-stealing, all-too-prevalent affliction. In its milder forms it frequently goes unnoticed, undiagnosed and untreated. But in its more severe manifestations it can be incapacitating and in some cases even fatal. It attacks men and women, young and old, rich and poor. What is this malady of which we are speaking? It is depression.

The word ``depression'' means many things to many people. Everyone has ``blue'' moods now and then, and this is perfectly normal. Also, many events in one's life such as family problems, a financial setback, retirement, loss or separation from a loved one, etc. provoke normal, expected reactions of sadness and grief. Unless grief is excessive or prolonged it is not depression. When we speak of depression throughout this book, we are referring to an unhealthy condition that has gone beyond the bounds of normal mood changes and situational reactions.

The signs and symptoms of depression are many and varied. Usually the more severe the depression the more disrupting are the symptoms. In its mildest form depression may be experienced as a persistent feeling of sadness that seems to hang on without any apparent reason. Uncontrollable feelings of sadness, helplessness and despair are often the most obvious indicators of deeper depression, along with nagging negative thoughts and self blame. The person suffering from depression may also experience anxiety and irritability, a lack of interest in his or her usual activities and relationships, and a paralyzing inability to make even simple, everyday decisions. Physically, depression robs one of energy and creates an overwhelming lethargy and tiredness. Insomnia, loss of appetite, headaches and other bodily discomforts are also common. Spiritually, the person who suffers from depression is characteristically burdened down by feelings of guilt and sinfulness. This in turn leads some to feel cut off from God and from any experience of his goodness. The joy which one once knew disappears and in its place is a dark, cold emptiness. Prayer, if one is able to pray at all, come forth as a cry for mercy and for help: it is a prayer in darkness.

As human persons we are complex, multi-faceted beings. Each of us possesses a body, a mind and a spirit. No one part of our being is ever afflicted in isolation from the others. Though we may not be aware of it, when we are depressed, *all* of the levels of our being are touched by depression. Depression, then, has biological-medical aspects, it has emotional-psychological aspects, and it has spiritual aspects. Depression affects the whole person.

No one (no matter how alone one may feel) is totally isolated from other persons. All of us live out our lives within a vast network of inter-connected roles and relationships. Each of us is constantly interacting with the world in which we live. When we are depressed our whole life feels its effects—our play, our work, our friendships, our marriage and family, and our community life. When we talk about depression we must also talk about it in this larger, social context. Depression afflicts our whole life as well as our whole person.

The perspectives on depression and its healing which are reflected throughout this book have largely grown out of the experiences and philosophy of the authors. In our own lives and in our work with others we have long been concerned with the problem of depression. Before proceeding any further, we would like to introduce ourselves. It is our hope that by sharing a glimpse of our backgrounds—particularly our personal experiences with depression—we can establish an atmosphere of openness and empathy which we believe is essential for the healing of depression.

I (Dick) am a Roman Catholic priest, ordained in 1963. All through seminary training and during these years of active ministry as a psychologist, teacher, and university administrator, I have experienced a deep, abiding satisfaction with my vocation in life and with my work. My efforts have been continually "rewarded" by promotions both in service to my religious community and at the university. I would characterize myself to be, in the eyes of others, a hard-working, caring and energetic person. Others, including my own family, would be surprised to know that I suffer from mild depression. For years I have successfully hidden my personal feelings of weakness and sadness along with other misgivings about myself. The ability to busy myself so completely in ministry or work has focused my attention outward and away from the inner, perplexing pain of depression. Those of us who successfully "mask" our depression generally seem able to organize and manage our lives rather effectively. However, an unexpected blow to our "well groomed" self-image can suddenly change all this. The following personal incident is an example.

The day began like any other. Little did I know that it would end with such pain. I was standing in the kitchen talking with two of the other men with whom I lived. The conversation turned toward me. Apparently one of the men, a very close and trusted friend, had decided that I needed to be made aware of my shortcomings; he proceeded, quite systematically, to criticize one aspect of my life after another until when he was finished almost every part of my life—23 things in all, everything from how I looked to the way I said Mass—had been judged and pronounced unsatisfactory.

I was taken totally by surprise. There had been no indication or warning that this was coming. As he talked I literally slumped to the floor as I felt my orderly world collapsing beneath me. I had so trusted my "image" into the care of these close friends that when the "rug was pulled out from under me" I took a very serious fall. Utterly dumbfounded, I could summon no response nor did I attempt to defend myself in the face of this massive repudiation of my person.

When my friend was finished I did the only thing I could think to do: I left the house and went to my office at the university. There I secluded myself for the next three days, leaving the office only to teach my classes. Because my friend had never been my student he had not attacked my teaching along with his other criticisms. Interestingly, this was literally the only area in which I was able to continue to function as usual. During these days of withdrawal I felt the full impact of what was perhaps the greatest rejection of my life. The overwhelming feelings of those days was hurt, which thoroughly permeated my consciousness. I made a list of the 23 items which had constituted my friend's comprehensive critique and I went over and over these in the next few days. Self-doubt, rigorous self-examination, helplessness, mourning, confusion, and a sense of betrayal had filled me. There seemed at the time to be no escape from this immense sadness and pain. Thoughts of taking my own life arose unbidden in my mind, and these utterly terrified me.

The loving but awkward support of other concerned friends was of invaluable help during these days. It has never been my way to be open in sharing my personal problems with others or to ask for help. Fortunately, I had two friends who didn't wait for an unlikely invitation to be of help. They literally invited themselves into my pain. I remember being grateful for their loving concern and thoughtfulness, but I was unable to summon words or find a way to hide my hurt and to erase their uneasiness. One of these friends stopped by my office that first evening to visit briefly and to bring me bread and wine and other things I would need in case I should wish to celebrate the Eucharist in the morning (which I found myself unable to do.) She and the other friend—who, incidentally, had been present as an observer during the confrontation at the house—checked me from time to time. Somehow I knew that I was not alone and I was loved. But knowing is not the same as feeling. I felt utterly isolated.

My prayer during this time was a weak but repeated "Help me, Lord." It was as though I was at the bottom of the sea, cut off and insulated from any spiritual consolation. Psalm 40, which has been a sustaining "theme" word in my adult life, came to mind again and again and was some source of strength. Otherwise, though, scripture which had always been so nourishing became dry and unconsoling. My heart was not filled with the forgiveness I have preached so often. Years later I still find my "hidden" self wounded with memories of resentments that cannot be "wished away" despite unspoken and spoken signs of repentance from my friends and forgiveness from me.

On the third day my two friends visited my office and insisted that I go out with them. We first stopped at a restaurant for ice cream. When we were finished we drove to a peaceful spot not far from there, ironically a cemetery. There my friends prayed with me for the inner healing of the wounds received a few days earlier.

The next day I began to see some light and feel some warmth radiating into my darkness and I sensed that resurrection was surely going to follow the days of isolation and suffering. The brief depression lifted almost as suddenly as it had been provoked. I look back on the experience as an extremely painful and memorable episode of depression in my life.

I (Chris) lead a busy but rewarding and fulfilling life. A single woman, I find my days and evenings are filled with variety of activities—a full-time job at the university, the vigorous pursuit of graduate studies, writing, counseling, and enjoying my sisters and their growing families. I am deeply satisfied with what and where I am at this time in my life, and look towards the future with optimism and anticipation. But things were not always this way. . . .

As I think back over the years it is hard for me to recall many periods in my life when I was not depressed. I was first hospitalized for depression when I was 17. That year (my senior year of high school) was a bad one for me, so much so in fact that my doctor insisted that I withdraw from school and complete my studies with a home tutor. Altogether, I was hospitalized seven times for psychiatric treatment of severe depression before I was 22 years old.

Feelings of hopelessness, guilt, deprivation, loneliness and intense frustration characterized my depressions. Living became so painful for me that I tried to escape by withdrawing inside myself. (I still fight the tendency to withdraw even now.) My withdrawal, however, brought consequences which made life all the more miserable for me. I made a number of suicide attempts—one of them almost successful—but these almost always resulted in hospitalization, leaving me further labelled as "sick," stripped of privileges, and less capable than before of coping with life.

One episode which was typical of my illness occurred in the fall term of my junior year of nursing studies. As usual there was no clear reason for my depression, which was accompanied by total mental and physical exhaustion. I had no energy to carry out even the simplest tasks for myself or my patients. Some mornings I just didn't bother to get up at all, choosing to stay in bed with the covers pulled over my head. I lost interest in everything—my studies, school activities, my friends, and my family.

Early in the term my roommate reached the limits of her tolerance. My uncommunicative attitude, my lack of interest in the usual campus and dorm activities, and my daytime sleeping behavior made living with me difficult (to say the least) and our friendship was irreparably damaged. At the time I couldn't understand Roberta's reaction, and I was terribly hurt by her lack of understanding and concern. My other friends avoided me, although I barely noticed this because I spent most of my time in seclusion. I felt terribly alone and misunderstood but I was completely unable to recognize the fact that I brought much of my misery down upon myself by my withdrawal and antisocial behavior.

For the first time in my entire life I started doing poorly with my academic work. I just couldn't concentrate, neither could I seem to understand or remember even the most basic material. I gave up trying to study. By the end of the term my grade point average plunged from 3.6 to 1.5, pushing me even further into despair. My grades in school had always been extremely important to me, and I was embarrassed and terribly upset by this sign of failure. The final blow came when the Dean of the School of Nursing forced me to take a leave of absence from my studies. Things were rapidly going from bad to worse. Against my will I was hospitalized for treatment.

Based on repeated psychiatric evaluations over the next four months, the administrators of the School of Nursing made the decision that I would not be allowed to continue my studies in professional nursing. This was, without a doubt, the biggest disappointment in my life. I still struggle at times with the pain of my ruined nursing career.

The above incident took place in late 1969 and early 1970. Beginning in 1964, however, I suffered an average of two such major depressive episodes every year until late in 1971. During that year I was working as an office nurse for a physician. In spite of my excellent adjustment as a paraprofessional, I remained depressed and deeply dissatisfied with my life. Spiritually, I had cast aside my Christian faith and turned to the occult in my search for meaning. This only deepened my confusion and despair, believing that only in death would I ever find the peace for which I so desperately longed. One night in October, after dialing a "wrong number," I became acquainted with a young priest who, without resorting to any "hard-sell" preaching which had so often hardened my heart in the past, quietly but powerfully revealed to me the loving, healing peace of Jesus. Although I was skeptical that God would share this peace with me, I realized that I had nothing to lose—things could not be worse—and so, in the dark of night in an empty church, with the young priest as my witness, I knelt before God, asked for his forgiveness and healing, and invited him to be Lord and Master of my life. Beginning that moment, a sense of joy and new life took root within me, and the healing of my rebellion, confusion, and depression began in earnest.

With this renewal of my faith came a growing trust in other persons. New, rich friendships developed, which I believe were vital to my healing. I became more active physically, intellectually socially and spiritually. I continued to see my psychiatrist for another four months, at which time he agreed that I was well on my way to recovery from the debilitating, severe depression which had caused me so much suffering over the years.

Although the depression has never returned with the crippling force it used to have, I still struggle with it at times and am thankful for the antidepressant medication which helps to keep it under control. I have not been hospitalized for depression since 1970.

Our stories which we have recounted here perhaps illustrate somewhat the different forms which depression may take. Hopefully they have also given you, the reader, a brief glimpse of who we are and where we have been. The experience of depression has not been a foreign or unknown one for either of us, and this fact has certainly contributed to our decision to undertake the writing of this book.

Memories like those we have included here linger through our lives no matter how healed we become. Among Christ's disciples the memories of his tragic passion and death must have been called up when he appeared to them after the resurrection with wounds in his hands and side. The Risen Christ did not hide these healed wounds; he even urged the apostle Thomas to touch them and to believe. The gospels tell us that healing will not lift the experience of suffering and the cross from our lives; rather, Christ will strengthen us to bear our burdens with understanding and wisdom.

There are many, many different approaches to the healing of depression. Although some combine one or more theories and methods, most of these approaches concentrate on one particular aspect of depression. There are medical (physical) therapies which attack the biochemical, physiological bases of depression. These medical therapies include various kinds of medication, electroshock therapy, special diets, vitamin treatments, exercise programs, and relaxation training. On the other hand, some treatment programs work primarily on the psychological causes of depression. There are many different kinds of individual and group psychotherapies. Depending on the theoretical orientation of the therapist, psychological therapies may delve into early childhood experiences, traumatic events, and conflicts which lie buried in one's unconscious mind. Other psychological approaches minimize the effects of past experiences and concentrate instead on one's present thinking patterns and habits, one's current interpersonal relationships, social skills, and activity levels. There are also spiritual approaches to the healing of depression. Some of these emphasize the inner healing of painful memories; others, the loving support of Christian community; still others rely on the powerfully healing effects of the sacraments, instruction in scripture and Christian teaching, prayer and the laying on of hands, and in some religious groups, prayer for deliverance from evil spirits.

Unfortunately, not all who are depressed avail themselves of the treatment that is available. The sad truth is that too often the person suffering from a heavy burden of depression withdraws within himself and cannot or will not ask for help. Some may throw themselves into their work or submerge themselves in a flurry of activities in their attempts to deny or to distract themselves from their distress. For those who do ask for help, often the first professional person to which they turn is the family physician. In many instances the family doctor can effectively treat mild depression, and the person will need to go no further in his search for help. Sometimes, however, the depressed person may be referred to a psychiatrist, clinical psychologist, or specially-trained social worker for specialized professional care. Instead of choosing a medical route to help, some persons may turn first to a priest, minister, rabbi or pastoral counselor. Others may seek out ''healing ministries,'' staffed by lay persons, which are developing in more and more churches and prayer communities today. More often than not, however, before looking for professional assistance the depressed person expresses his unhappiness to a family member or close friend.

This book has grown out of a deep and profound concern for those whose lives have been wounded by depression. As our stories indicate, both of us have waged our own personal battles against the freedom-thief of depression. But perhaps more motivating than this has been our experience with people who are hurting—not only people who are depressed, but their spouses, families and friends who are struggling with them to understand and to be freed from this very common but serious problem. It is primarily for these people—those who are depressed and those who are striving to understand and help those who are depressed—that we have written this book.

As you make your way through the pages of this book, you will encounter, hopefully, not only an intellectual understanding of depression but also an emotional and spiritual insight into what it means to be depressed. Some people suffer from mild forms of masked depression in their lives which they themselves do not recognize. Possibly for these persons this book may facilitate greater self-understanding and, we hope, healing of this often hidden source of woundedness.

It is not our wish to merely duplicate the many volumes on depression which already exist. In the past several years an enormous number of books have been written about this illness. Many of these are limited to a single perspective; thus one can find books that very amply cover the psychological approach to depression, others that are devoted to the medical theory and treatment of depression, and still others which reflect the orientation towards "natural" or "folk" remedies. There are several books available which are written specifically from a spiritual, Christian viewpoint. The problem that we have encountered with the majority of these books is that they are (1) all psychology with no attention given to the spiritual elements of depression and healing, or (2) many of the spiritual books are narrow in their approach to the subject, rejecting or overlooking valid and valuable insights offered by modern medical and psychological science.

Because depression is such a multi-dimensional problem, we are convinced that the more effective approaches to healing will be those designed to heal the whole person. We offer this book, then, in an effort to provide an integrated, holistic approach to the understanding and treatment of depression. We have endeavored to unite medical-biological, emotional-psychological, and spiritual approaches to depression, all within the context of Christian faith. Great care has been taken to write in as clear and straightforward a style as possible without at the same time "watering down" important ideas. It is our hope that this book will be of help not only to those who suffer from depression but also to the family members, friends, and others who are striving to help those who are depressed.

PSALM 40

A PRAYER FOR HELP

I have waited, waited for the Lord,
and he stooped toward me and heard my cry.
He drew me out of the pit of destruction,
out of the mud of the swamp;
He set my feet upon a crag, he made firm my steps.
And he put a new song into my mouth, a hymn to our God.
Many shall look on in awe and trust in the Lord.
Happy the man who makes the Lord his trust.

Withhold not, O Lord, your compassion from me;
may your kindness and your truth ever preserve me.
For all about me are evils beyond reckoning;
my sins so overcome me that I cannot see.
They are more numerous than the hairs of my head,
and my heart fails me.

Deign, O Lord, to rescue me; O Lord, make haste to help me.
Let all be put to shame and confusion
who seek to snatch away my life.
But may all who seek you exult and be glad in you,
And may those who love your salvation
say ever, "The Lord be glorified."
Though I am afflicted and poor, yet the Lord thinks of me.
You are my help and my deliverer, O my God, hold not back!

CHAPTER TWO

THE HELPLESSNESS OF DEPRESSION

Just what is depression? What exactly are we speaking of when we say that someone suffers from depression? The word "depression" is commonly used in ordinary conversation to refer to anything from a momentary disappointment or a short-lived "blue mood," to a serious condition requiring hospitalization. In her book *I'm Dancing as Fast as I can*[1] Barbara Gordon writes: "I had thought depression meant simply sadness. I didn't know one *felt* crazed, insane, dumb, dead, numb, enraged, hysterical, all at once. Depression is a killer." Obviously there is a world of difference between the usually happy and energetic individual who occasionally feels a little low and less enthusiastic than usual and the individual who is painfully depressed to the point where he or she is unable or barely able to carry out ordinary daily responsibilities. While not denying the unpleasantness of an occasional blue mood, when we speak of depression we are referring to something more than this. Specifically, we are speaking of depressed feelings and behavior which along with associated physical problems interfere with one's ability to feel good about one's life, to perceive one's situation accurately and realistically, and to interact well with other persons.

You will note that this definition is not limited just to individuals who are hurting so much that they are suicidal or "out of control.'' Certainly people who are so desperately unhappy that they contemplate taking their own lives are depressed. But in many instances—fortunately—depression does not lead to such a crisis point. Many people, in fact, do not think of themselves as suffering from depression because the notion of ''depression'' conjures up images of tearful women, slashed wrists, and perhaps even mental hospitals. The fact is, though, that authorities estimate that at any given moment approximately eight million Americans are in immediate need of professional help for depression, and only a very small minority of these are in need of hospitalization.

Perhaps it would clarify things a bit if we describe depression in terms of its acute and chronic forms. Acute depression, as the name implies, is usually of sudden onset but of relatively short duration. Often depression of this type is a reaction to very stressful external circumstances. An acute depressive reaction is marked by unavoidable feelings of abandonment, hopelessness, anguish and anxiety. The acutely depressed person may have trouble sleeping, often loses his or her appetite, has difficulty concentrating, and frequently becomes inactive and reclusive. Life loses its color and there seems to be no future worth living. Many acutely depressed people are able to identify the event or situation which precipitated their depression, although they usually cannot explain why their response is so exaggerated or prolonged. Some acute depressions become severe enough to warrant hospitalization when there is a danger of suicide. Even in severe cases, however, the prognosis is good; although the depression may persist for weeks or even months, in most cases it will clear up on its own and life returns to normal once again.

Chronic depression, on the other hand, can almost be thought of as a way of life. In fact, the word ''chronic'' technically refers to a relatively permanent pattern or condition. Many chronic depressives, who suffer the same core symptoms common to the acute depressive, cannot recall a time in their life when they were not depressed. Even so, no one really becomes accustomed to being depressed all of the time, but chronically depressed people have usually learned how to function in spite of their depression. In general, chronically depressed individuals are very unhappy people who have lost their zest for life and find little joy in their own accomplishments or their relationships with others.

For those suffering from depression and those who are close to them, this illness remains such an exasperating mystery; it is very difficult to find words to define just what the problem is. With most sicknesses and surgery there is a typical "down time," the illness is visible, and it is discussable. With depression none of these seem to apply. When you break an arm you can blame it on something or find a cause. Depression, on the other hand, has remained a painful mystery for which neither problems nor solutions are easily identifiable.

One of the hallmarks of depression, whether it be acute or chronic, is the paralyzing sense of helplessness which so often accompanies it. Some depressed persons remark that they feel powerless to change the situation in which they find themselves. There appear to be no alternatives from which to choose. Wherever they turn they see closed doors and roadblocks shutting them off from happiness. Minor barriers now have become insurmountable obstacles. Depressed persons often say that they feel closed off from life and hopelessly chained to their depression. Much of the painfulness of depression comes fom this perceived loss of control over one's life. Though initially they may make some attempts to lift themselves from depression, too often depressed individuals seemingly give up hope and become passive and resigned.

Many depressions are the result of events or circumstances in the life of the individual. These external precipitators of depression may include such things as terminal illness, death of a loved one, divorce, chronic pain, and many other uncontrollable, life-altering situations which destroy one's dreams and plans for the future. In all of these painful, disrupting events the individual is confronted with loss and change. We all know persons who have experienced such life stresses yet have not become depressed. Thus it is very important to remember that it is not so much the objective or external significance of the event which causes a depressive reaction, but the subjective or inner significance which the event has for the individual. For example, Bill and Susan each experience the loss of a close friend after a serious disagreement. Although the objective, external event may be the same for them both, the subjective inner consequences may be vastly different. A low level of self-confidence plus a history of more failures than successes in life may lead Bill to react to the event with a feeling of helplessness, an attitude that concludes: "It's hopeless. When things like this have happened to me before, everything I tried went wrong. So I'm sure there's absolutely nothing I can do to change it." Susan successfully adjusts to the interpersonal difficulty while Bill becomes paralyzed by depression and self-blame.

Dr. Martin Seligman, a psychologist researcher, developed a theory[2] in which he describes depression as "learned helplessness." During some experiments in the laboratory, Seligman discovered that when dogs were placed in a box and given a mild, annoying but harmless electric shock on their paws which they could not escape, they first struggled and barked as they tried to avoid the irritating shock. When they were later placed in a box where all they had to do to escape shock was to jump over a low barrier, however, the dogs merely cowered passively and whimpered, making no attempt at all to escape the uncomfortable shock. Seligman attributed this finding to the fact that the dogs had learned that there was nothing they could do to avoid the shock; they had developed the habit of being helpless. It was as if they had said to themselves, "Why even try?"

Dr. Seligman found it interesting to note that the dogs' helpless behavior was very much like that of persons who suffer from depression. From these studies and others which came later, Seligman and a number of other investigators in the area of human depression have developed the theory that depression results from learning, through a series of bad experiences, that one is unable to control what happens to him. In other words, one aspect of depression is learned helplessness. It appears that helplessness may be both a cause and an effect of depression. The cure for depression begins when the individual is able to believe that he is not helpless.

All depressed persons seem to experience a decrease in their self-confidence, that is, their inner feelings of being a worthwhile, valuable and lovable person. Persons with low self-confidence are much more vulnerable to depression—particularly a severe depression—than are persons who feel good about themselves. Many events of daily life which do not match with one's hopes further decrease self-confidence as well as serving as confirmation that the individual is "no good." This negative way of interpreting events is a direct result of distorted perception, as we will see in the next chapter. In our example above, Bill, who deep down already felt undeserving of respect and love, interpreted the conflict with his friend as further proof that this was true. This episode is filed away in his memory along with other memories of rejection. His level of self-confidence is now lower than it was before.

With his freshly reaffirmed vision of himself as unworthy and unlovable Bill begins to lose interest and to withdraw. A frequent response to decreased self-confidence, loss of interest and withdrawal result in a self-imposed separation from other persons, God and life in general. The depressed individual, inwardly fearful of more rejection and misunderstanding than he has already suffered, almost without realizing it distances himself from family, friends, co-workers and even God. Often the depressed person is not conscious of the reasons for his withdrawal. For instance, Bill finds himself more and more preferring to stay at home watching television than going bowling with friends or attending a PTA meeting with his wife. At the office his co-workers notice that Bill seems unusually quiet and distant. At home he puts the kids off when they want to play. His wife is concerned about Bill's apparent lack of interest in the activities which were formerly so important to him. It is as if an invisible wall has been built around him.

One inevitable result of this kind of loss of interest and withdrawal is guilt and self-blame which add to the problem rather than decrease it. Bill's distancing of himself creates feelings of guilt: he chastises himself for not being the husband, father and friend that he believes he should be. These guilt feelings in turn confirm his picture of himself as "no good" and undeserving of love and respect. Self-confidence hits a new low ebb. The vicious cycle just keeps on going, with his further decreased self-confidence leading to greater withdrawal, which produces more feelings of guilt. . .and so on.

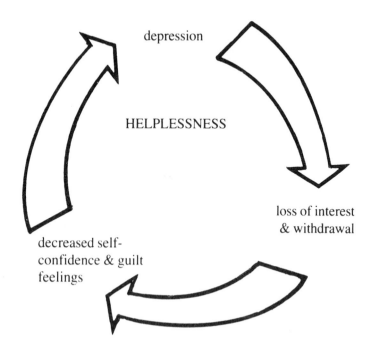

depression

HELPLESSNESS

loss of interest
& withdrawal

decreased self-
confidence & guilt
feelings

Caught up in this cycle, the depressed person feels totally helpless. None of his actions seem effective and so he ''retires.'' It seems that he is at the mercy of a force far more powerful than he, a force he cannot seem to understand or find the energy to overcome. It is as though he is being pulled further and further downward in a spiraling whirlpool of depression.

Just as a drowning man needs the help of a lifeguard, so does the depressed person need the help of others. In the same sense a person who has been immobilized by feelings of helplessness needs the listening ear and helping hand of an empathetic friend.

First of all, it is extremely difficult to listen to someone who is experiencing deep inner anguish or depression. The one who does listen also may be overwhelmed with feelings of helplessness, wondering, ''How can I ever be of any help in this dismal situation?'' In fact, after much listening, it is even hard to comprehend what the problem is. Secondly, most of us have a strong desire to repair that which lies broken in front of us. Because our spouses, friends and associates are so precious to us, we become both anxious and eager to jump in and to fix the problems and hurts of depression suffered by those we love. The perplexing truth is that no matter what is tried, whether it be a standard solution or a religious solution, nothing seems to work. Our resourcefulness at finding ''solutions'' scarcely seems to be appreciated or to alleviate the depression.

One common human response is to give up all effort to communicate with someone who is withdrawn behind such impenetrable walls. It is not difficult to understand why people give up trying to reach out to the one suffering from depression—so seldom is there a supportive response in return. And thus, the depressed person experiences family and friends fading from view when help from others is most needed.

Another human response to a depressed friend or family member is to keep listening. This kind of listening should refrain from offering easy solutions since they are not received as helpful.

It is so frustrating for the listener when one cannot be of any help. And so in the midst of all this listening, the depressed person often experiences a very frustrated spouse, friend or associate. There seems to be little the depressed person can do to make life more pleasant for this devoted, listening person.

Another response to depression is to help. What does it mean to help another? The dictionary definition tells us that help means to supply another with whatever is necessary to accomplish *his* ends or relieve *his* wants. A key word here is *his*. Too often helping another involves a helper's shift to serving his or her own ends or wants by doing what the *helper* thinks is needed. I (Chris) can remember calling up a friend when I was very depressed; I wanted and needed to spend time with a patient, listening friend. Instead, my friend had all kinds of other ideas about what I *really* needed. What would really help me, my friend insisted, was to be with a group of people: a party, a potluck, or a prayer meeting was just the thing I needed to lift me out of my depression. The last thing in the world that I wanted to do was to put on my ''mask'' and try to be happy and sociable when I was hurting so much inside. My friend's well-intentioned but insensitive ''help'' left me feeling all the more helpless, misunderstood and depressed. As helpers many of us are not alert to this subtle, self-serving tendency in ourselves. This is most difficult for someone requesting help, especially for the depressed person experiencing helplessness. A plea for help signifies some loss of one's treasured sense of independence and confirms all the more one's powerlessness. When the helper's response to this plea is primarily self-serving, the person in need is left frustrated by unmet needs and with deeper feelings of his or her inability to communicate well with others. It is unlikely one suffering from depression will ask the self-serving helper for assistance soon again!

An effective approach for those developing in the art of helping may be termed ''pure caring.'' This kind of caring is expressed in the following attitude: ''I care enough about you that I want this help to be what you need rather than what I want.'' Such caring involves listening, reflection, humility and action. Beneath the words of one's spoken request for help there often lie many more unspoken needs. Thus, our *listening* must be sensitive. Without a genuine effort to listen carefully and to know the person better, these deeper needs will probably remain unnoticed and undiscussed. The second requirement for pure caring involves *reflection* on what we have heard and how best to provide help. When possible some thought and prayer should be devoted to the best way to preserve the other's dignity and self-confidence when help is given. Time taken for this reflection opens the way for wisdom and understanding. *Humility* is the third requirement for the helper. Self-seeking desires and attitudes of superiority can blind us to the real felt needs of others. In effect, such attitudes put us in the dangerous position of judging ourselves as more capable of determining needs and solutions for others. Finally, after listening, reflection and setting aside our own ''better'' solutions, pure caring requires *giving what is requested* if it is physically, emotionally and morally possible to do so. If for some reason we are unable to provide the help requested, we should honestly communicate this to the person asking for help.

Recently at a retreat, I (Dick) presented this model for pure caring during one of the conferences. I used the example of needing and asking for food—two cans of tomato sauce—to be used with a turkey dinner I was preparing. Several retreatants immediately began to laugh. One suddenly suggested I really needed cranberry sauce, not tomato sauce; another remarked I obviously knew nothing about cooking! Interestingly, even in this context of ''pure caring'' I was both denied tomato suace and judged inadequate in the kitchen! How often the person suffering from depression faces this frustrating kind of experience from well meaning helpers.

In the midst of the paralyzing, frustrating helplessness experienced by the depressed person, what can be done beyond providing some pure caring? Before any more steps can be taken.

the root problem must be identified. Once the problem is identified as depression, an important move has been made in the direction of recovery. For some people this is a very difficult thing to do. Many common misconceptions about the nature of depression lead people to react with fear or with shame to the suggestion that their problem is indeed depression. It must be realized, however, that whenever we can identify a thing and call it by name we cease to be helpless victims and begin to assume some control over the matter. This acceptance is crucial. It is for this reason that Alcoholics Anonymous, for instance, has developed the very powerful tradition seen at every AA meeting anywhere in the world in which members introduce themselves, ''My name is $------$ and I am an alcoholic.'' The identification and naming of depression paves the way for the next steps in the healing journey.

Why is this so important? It is essential for the very simple reason that one cannot change something—in this case the helplessness, guilt and withdrawal of depression—until one becomes convinced that there is something that does indeed need changing. One must confront the depression by admitting it to oneself. As many AA members have discovered, it is often also necessary to tell another person of one's problem. Anytime we undertake a self-change project, whether it be dieting, striving to become physically fit, or overcoming depression, it is easier to keep at it if we have someone to encourage us. Also, when we know that someone else is aware and supportive of our efforts, we are more motivated to keep working.

Enlisting the help of a family member or close friend is helpful for another reason. As we have seen, a major factor in the cycle of helplessness and depression is withdrawal and loss of interest in one's usual activities. When we are depressed we tend to avoid others. This withdrawal raises new guilt feelings which in the long run keep us depressed—stuck in the vicious cycle. Loss of interest and withdrawal is the weakest link in the cycle, and thus the very best place to begin the attack against depression. It is difficult to work on low self-confidence or guilt feelings directly; we can't see them or measure them or "adjust" them in a direct manner. We *can* directly deal with our action or lack of action, though. If we can do something about our withdrawal, even if only by confiding in and seeking the listening ear of an understanding friend, guilt feelings about loss of interest and withdrawal will begin to subside and we will begin to sense a new interest in ourselves and in the things going on around us.

The need for others is so important that it can't be overemphasized. Even though others are gentle and loving, it is still hard to communicate to them what one is experiencing—the helplessness and hopelessness, the fear and the guilt. And as we've said earlier, it is also frustrating for the listener to know that a loved one is struggling and suffering but yet not know how to help. Perhaps a descriptive image will shed some light on the situation.

We can picture the depressed person down in a deep pit. The pit is dark and cold and very isolated; it is frighteningly lonely. On all sides there are only rocky, muddy walls; there are no handholds nor solid footholds which would provide a way to climb up and out. Deep in the pit one is totally helpless and easily becomes resigned to days of darkness and despair. There seems to be no way of escape. This is how it feels when one has sunk in the depths of depression: one feels overwhelmed and imprisoned by nagging but deadly feelings of worthlessness, fear and self-blame. Concerned friends or family members stand above on the edge of the pit, yearning to help. Even so, it's very hard to call for help from the paralyzing helplessness of depression. Sometimes it's even difficult to admit to others that you're even down there.

The initiative must often be taken by someone willing to provide pure caring by listening patiently and non-judgmentally. In this way the helper can provide a ladder of support and love which can be lowered into the pit. When the helper offers this help, the depressed person may very well react with fear and doubt. Then questions like these crowd into his mind: "Can I trust this rescuer to know and understand what I am experiencing? Is he able to help me? Will he rush me or will he give me time to climb the ladder at my own pace? If I cannot bring myself to accept this offer right now, will he abandon me and never return?'' So often when one is depressed, help is fervently desired yet at the same time fearfully avoided.

Offering help to the person who is depressed requires immense patience and understanding. It may be a long time before one is able to accept the care that is offered. The healing of helplessness and depression ultimately depends upon one's willingness and ability to trust others and God. Until one trusts, one cannot climb up the ladder and out of the pit. Perhaps the hardest thing for helpers to understand is that they cannot go down into the pit, grab ahold of the person, and carry him up the ladder. The decision and the courage to climb up that ladder must come from the one in the pit. It can be no other way. The depressed person must climb the ladder himself, and though others may offer love, encouragement and support, they cannot do it for him. They can, however, provide the encouragement which may help to mobilize the depressed person out of his passive state of helplessness so that he can gradually, one step at a time climb the ladder and come out of the pit.

In the gospel of John (5:1-15) we read of the cure of the sick man. He was lying among many sick people by the pool of Bethzatha whose waters were said to have curative effects when stirring by God's angel. The man had been ill for 38 years and he spent considerable time and energy seeking a cure. But he needed help; he could not accomplish his healing alone. When Jesus saw the man lying there, he knew the man had suffered for many years. Jesus asked him, ''Do you want to be well again?'' The helpless man responded that he was unable to get into the curative waters before other sick people, and thus he did not receive a cure. Our reaction, in the spirit of pure caring, probably would be to help this man who had sufffered and waited so long. Helping him would involve assisting him, as he would request, to the pool before the others seeking cures. And he may have been healed of his illness. At the very least he would have established a new helpful relationship with someone willing and able to listen and to respond lovingly. Jesus' response was even more direct and penetrating. He simply said, ''Get up, pick up your sleeping mat and walk.'' John tells us the man was cured at once and he picked up his mat and walked away.

The sick or depressed person scarcely imagines himself or herself as a healed or changed person. One does not ordinarily ask for what is unimaginable or seems impossible. Such is the condition of helplessness. But God has a way of knowing and reaching to the depths of helplessness. He responds to our weak pleas with powerful divine favor never dreamt possible.

> Yahweh is an everlasting God,
> He created the boundaries of the earth.
> He does not grow tired or weary,
> His understanding is beyond fathoming.
> He gives strength to the wearied,
> He strengthens the powerless.
> Young men may grow tired and weary,
> Youths may stumble,
> But those who hope in Yahweh renew their strength,
> They put out wings like eagles.
> They run and do not grow weary,
> Walk and never tire.
>
> (Is 40:28-31).

Footnotes

1. Barbara Gordon, *I'm Dancing As Fast As I Can* (New York: Bantam Books, 1980), p. 151.
2. M.E.P. Seligman, *Helplessness* (San Francisco: W.H. Freeman, 1975).

CHAPTER   THREE

THE DISTORTION OF DEPRESSION

It is difficult for the helpless person to see out of the pit, and when we are "blind" from depression, lacking vision and hope, the contours of life lose their clarity. Among the many complicated pathways of the brain's sensing-thinking-perceiving apparatus, what really *is* becomes altered and distorted when we are depressed. Also, how we feel is intimately related to how we see our world. In order to understand the "blindness" of depression we must turn our attention to the mental process of perception.

As we experience our world from moment to moment we are constantly gathering sensory information. We put this information together with our memories of the past to "make sense" of our present situation. This process, which is called *perception*, is much more than just passive seeing, hearing, smelling, tasting and touching. Perception is the mental process through which our memories and our present experiences blend what we are sensing into a *meaningful* whole. Thus, each person's perception of something is indeed unique.

An example of the *personal* quality of our perception is the different ways the authors see and find meaning in the cross. While we both *see* the cross as it is, the interesting thing is that we each *perceive* something different; in other words, while we see the same cross, neither of us has the same perception.

When Dick looks at the cross he perceives a powerful, symbolic image. The cross for Dick is a meaningful, ever-present element in his daily life. ''If you wish to follow me, take up your cross daily'' (Mk 8:34). The cross for him symbolizes an active call: it is a call to keep working despite how he feels. Dick's perception is in accord with his approach to life. He is the kind of person we term a ''workaholic'' because he staves off much of the pain of his depression by immersing himself in activity.

Busy with his teaching, administrative and ministerial responsibilities, Dick treasures the words of Jesus: ''Whatsoever you *do* to the least of these, you *do* unto me'' (Mt 25:40). Dick's characteristic way of approaching life colors his perception of the cross: it becomes for him the cross that he is called to recognize and to carry to others in his daily work and ministry.

Chris, on the other hand, perceives the cross in a different way. As one who suffers from chronic depression, Chris is intimately familiar with the shadow of the cross as it falls upon her life. For her it is a symbol of all of the heartache, struggle and disappointment which life brings. Chris looks upon the cross as something which must be accepted and endured. In sharp contrast to the workaholic, Chris' response is one of passivity and resignation. The cross for her is much like the inescapable shock which made Dr. Seligman's laboratory dogs become so helpless. Rather than perceiving the cross as that which one is called to bear, the cross is instead perceived as the symbol of all in life that is unbearable.

Although the cross for Chris means suffering, she trusts in God's promise that he is always near, for to live with the presence of the cross is to live in the presence of Jesus. Daily she finds strength in this word of Scripture: ''For I am convinced that there is nothing in death or life . . . , no heights nor depths—nothing in all creation that can separate us from the love of God made visible in Christ Jesus our Lord'' (Rm 8:38-39). Nothing—not even depression—can separate us from the love of God our Father.

How different these two perceptions are! One could, for example, label the first one "Healthy" and the second one "Sick." After all, the "workaholic" seems by all appearances to be strong, responsible, and in accord with God's will. The openly depressed person, on the other hand, appears weak and passive. There is no doubt that the person who uses constant activity as a defense against his or her depression is much more likely to be perceived by others as a "good" Christian. The passive individual, on the other hand, projects a picture of weakness and he or she may be perceived by others as a "bad" Christian. But the truth is that all depression, no matter how expressed or hidden, is no doubt viewed by God as a burden or trial for those he loves. As Scripture says, "God does not see as man sees; man looks at appearances, but Yahweh looks at the heart" (1 S 16:7). While each of us may perceive different meanings in the cross, for the Lord himself that cross has a deeper, personal significance. As we identify more closely with him, he opens his perception to us. Words from Isaiah say:

> I will lead the blind on their journey; by paths unknown I will guide them. I will turn darkness into light before them, and make crooked ways straight. These things I do for them, and I will not forsake them (Is 42:16).

What a powerful message of love and hope the word of God brings us!

We have shared our differing perceptions of the cross in order to demonstrate how uniquely each of us perceives life. Normally a variety of factors influence perception, but when we are depressed our view of life is particularly vulnerable to distortion. We now turn our attention to some of the factors which are continually at work to alter and influence our perception.

In no situation are we ever separated from the influence of our past experience. To one degree or another, our memory for this past is also with us. Thus we always perceive, not with a blank mind but with a backlog of experience which gives *expectancy* to what we will see. This expectation—sometimes very conscious and at other times quite unconscious—has a very powerful effect on what we see and the meaning or interpretation we give it. As we receive the actual stimulus (sights, sounds, sequence of events, etc.) from a situation, our perceptual processes enable us to confirm or correct our expectations. If the reality of the situation is different from what we expected, this unfamiliar or contrary stimulus situation will have to be quite strong in order to win out over our expectations and to be perceived accurately. Otherwise we are likely to see just what we expected or "wanted" to see.

Perception happens automatically. In fact, usually we are unaware of the extent to which we are constantly engaged in a process of selecting, choosing and filtering. Perception carries the conviction that what we see is a true and direct representation of reality. We believe and are ready to stand by what we see—or think we see. An illusion or false perception seems false only when reality is able to break through to us and we recognize it as truth.

A photographer, for example, through the use of different lenses or filters, can drastically alter the image of reality with his camera. What the camera sees and records on film may not be an accurate view of the world at all. A wide angle lens, for instance, encompasses the broad panorama but makes it appear smaller and more distant. A telephoto lens, on the other hand, sees reality with a much narrower, selective view; it may entirely shut out the sun and landscape as it focuses in on a thorn bush. A normal lens sees smiling friends, but a fish-eye lens distorts and transforms the same friends into grotesque beings. One type of filter blurs what is real; another filter fragments a subject into many partial and broken images; still other filters cast a pall of unreal darkness upon a scene, wrap it in mist, put stars in the heavens where there were none, or fool us into seeing six trees where there is really only one. Perspective, proportion, emphasis, tone, clarity, breadth and narrowness can all be changed. In fact, the very "heart of reality" can be totally altered and thus misperceived. Mechanical manipulations of the photographic equipment cause the camera to distort the real world. Our past experiences and memory of them, our physical condition and feelings, and our expectations act like the lenses or filters on the camera by "manipulating" reality as it is processed through our perceptual system.

Much like the distorted photographic view of life as seen through the filters and lenses of the camera, our view of the world and reality becomes altered when we are depressed. What we perceive the world to be may not be what it really is. The problem with the camera analogy, however, is that the photographer is very aware of the distortions in his work because he deliberately creates them; the depressed person, on the other hand, is most often unaware that what he or she is perceiving is not accurate or faithful to the truth. It is like being partially blind or very limited without realizing it.

Depression affects our perception of the world. It is like a set of filters which narrows our view, emphasizes the darker aspects of a situation, and eliminates action and warmth from the scene. The following excerpt from the journal of a depressed young woman provides an illustration of the way the world looks as seen through her eyes:

> I suppose the thing I recall most about some of my "bad spells" is the way life seemed to grind to an absolute halt. Or maybe it would be more accurate to say that it was like everything was in slow motion, dream-like. Every process just sort of slows way down: it requires immense effort to take a single step, to lift a fork, to put on clothes. There seems to be no energy left. Not only is there no energy for physical movement but there's likewise no energy for thought. The simplest mental processes become complex; it becomes impossible to make even the smallest decisions. From inside my head I looked out through my eyes on a gray-colored world. To say things are black is to give more credit than is due— there is simply no contrast. In its place is a monochromatic, silent, slowed-down world. . . .

The greater the intensity of the depression, the greater the distortion becomes. Life loses its color and excitement and becomes a dreary task to be endured rather than enjoyed. The world appears distant, uncaring, and alien. Depression leaves one feeling all alone in the midst of an impersonal world:

> I'm frustrated, confused . . .
> I feel as though I am
> Wavering on the far edge of hope,
> Any moment to fall forever
> Into darkness, into No-Man's Land.
>
> And I'm scared. . . .
> Perched in this precarious position,
> Not sure of anything,
> In touch with nothing—
> Not even myself.
>
> If I could be free
> Surely I'd be happy, then,
> If only I could get this
> Albatross off my neck,
> An albatross named me.
>
> Bring your lantern,
> Step into the depths
> Where no light shines
> No fire warms
> No one comes:
> Just me.

The filter of depression leaves the depressed person feeling that deep and urgent personal needs have been ignored or rejected by an unconcerned world. When depression distorts our perception we misinterpret the feelings and concern of others, including those closest to us. We feel that they have shut us out. And these others, our family, associates and friends, likewise feel shut out or "distanced" by us. Now, more than at any other time, when we want and need understanding, love and support, these others feel barred from providing them. While immersed in the totally absorbing world of depression it is difficult for the depressed person to perceive why friends and loved ones react as they do. Misunderstanding and withdrawal are the result.

The image of God also changes when one is depressed. One sees God as angry, uncaring and far away. A depression-distorted concept of God and self are dramatized in this journal entry:

I feel so guilty for how I feel, so ungrateful. On one hand I acknowledge how I think I *should* feel and believe, and on the other how I really *do* feel. The two are so different. "God loves me; He is good" vs. "God is silent, distant, apparently uninvolved, a spectator." I feel like someone vastly superior to me is detachedly watching, curious to see whether I will make it through this maze.

It's as though I were a laboratory rat. For the rat, the walls of the maze are tall and formidable barriers; perhaps the puzzle simply cannot be mastered by the poor animal. But for the observing scientist, from his perspective, those maze walls are very small indeed and from his vantage point the solution is so obvious that he wonders why the rat is so frustrated.

But the rat is a rat and will always be a rat. The perspective of the scientist will never be his. He is doomed to rathood and ratness for the remainder of his rat-life. The fear and confusion he experiences, the frustration expressed in his red rat-eyes, remain uncomforted by his foggy awareness that the ever-present scientist looms over him, possessing the answers, seeing the solution, but remaining distant. The scientist has a hundred rats and if this one is stupid, clumsy or crippled—well, there are plenty of other specimens of the rat race. The data concerning poor Rat is carefully recorded in the great scientific notebook, just one rat among thousands. But to that rat, those observations are so significant because they chronicle his Everything. He has only one rat-life and that life is all he's got.

>It's hard to believe in a loving and personal God who knows the answers and wants us to succeed and yet who seems to be afar off. . . .

Sometimes one is convinced there is an enormous wall separating oneself from God. It is hard to sense anything about God. It is hard to pray; words don't come easily and a brooding silence fills one's spirit. Even though we may know intellectually that God loves us, deep down we perceive ourselves unloved and abandoned. Sometimes anger erupts and one asks, "What right did God have to create me? Why is he doing this to me?" Depression distorted perception selectively screens out our awareness of the many instances of mercy and unconditional love of God, and focuses instead on judgment and punishment. It filters out his presence and warmth from our prayer and from the words of Scripture.

More distorted by depression is one's view of oneself. Convictions about one's personal worth and goodness seem to vanish from memory when depression descends. The sadness and helplessness of depression are fixed to the vision of oneself as unlovable, unattractive and inferior. Thus, the depressed person sees himself or herself as bad, worthless, and perhaps even evil. Such a dim view of oneself, when even minimally compared to reality and the expectations of others, *seems* "out of focus" and makes one feel wrong or guilty. Guilt for real, exaggerated or imagined transgressions can become an overwhelming source of pain. Actual weaknesses and mistakes are blown out of proportion and then held as proof that one is no good. This greatly distorted perception of self lies beneath many of the false perceptions of others and of God. A paralyzing feeling of helplessness to change oneself or one's situation is the result.

All of us are bombarded by the false values and expectations of our society. Advertising, television, popular music and even greeting cards inundate us with these messages: "I'm a good person IF I am physically attractive or have a magnetic and charming pesonality," and "I'm a good person IF I'm productive and successful."

Unfortunately, the unwitting acceptance of such cultural values has led many to lives of unreachable expectations, failure and self-condemnation. When one is depressed how easy it is—and how true it sounds—to say to oneself, "I'm not attractive; I am not a success. I am no good. I am worthless. I am unlovable." We come to expect rejection, for our expectations are unrealistic. We judge ourselves as the result of a false view of the world and a false perception of ourselves.

In addition to the expectation of our society, many of us also experience false expectations in our "faith community" or among those who are in our church family. Now and then "spiritual" expectations are distorted by false values. For example, when a person suffers from depression or from any kind of pain, the normal human response is not one of inner joy or happiness. On the contrary, mental, physical and spiritual suffering causes a deep discomfort from which one seeks relief or for which one seeks healing. Unfortunately, a false spiritual solution is sometimes offered to those who suffer. They are counseled to bear the ache or hurt silently and with a smile: "Recover from this suffering by denying it!" To urge one in pain to face life in this way amounts to asking for silent withdrawal when one is unable to escape the reality of pain. In effect, such false expectations ask a person to bear pain beneath a *mask* of false joy or apparent acceptance. *Holy* people are said to suffer silently and with joy. Such "courage," however, does not correspond to the experience of those in pain. Thus, filled with a greater sense of failure for one's lack of holiness or spirituality, the depressed person sees himself or herself as a sinner and unlovable. The result is even greater withdrawal from the help and healing which the faith community and God can bring. Even Jesus himself would not have measured up well to these false spiritual expectations. As he underwent the agony in the garden prior to his death, he was neither silent nor joyful; he asked his Father to release him from the burden of his suffering (Lk 22:42).

The only remedy for distorted perception is realistic perception. But how does one begin to see the world, God and oneself accurately? It is difficult for the depressed person to do this alone. The healing of depression, like most healing, does not occur in a vacuum; healing is not a private matter but a process in which others are involved. This is a time when we must *trust* others to help us see.

The writer of the Gospel of Mark records a beautiful example of how one man was healed and began to see:

> They came to Bethsaida, and some people brought to him a blind man whom they begged him to touch. He took the blind man by the hand and led him outside the village. Then putting spittle on his eyes and laying his hands on him, he asked "Can you see anything?" The man, who was beginning to see, replied, "I can see people; they look like trees to me, but they are walking about." Then he laid his hands on the man's eyes and he saw clearly; he was cured, and he could see everything plainly and distinctly (Mk 8:22-25).

The concerned friends of the blind man, knowing of his condition and the helplessness which he was experiencing, took the initiative and led him to Jesus. For his part, the blind man trusted the vision of his good friends and allowed them to lead him. Jesus, reaching into the world of this man who could not see, took him by the hand . . . laid his hands upon him. When the man's eyes were first opened he still misperceived. Jesus, with love and patience, again laid his hands upon him until at last he "saw clearly . . . he could see everything plainly and distinctly."

This story of the blind man is an example of the need for supportive relationships in the process of becoming whole. Anyone who has lived or worked with a depressed person knows, however, that remaining positive and supportive can be very difficult. We have a natural tendency to want to avoid someone who is depressed. We are perplexed by this kind of "emotional blindness." But more than that, depressed people frequently withdraw from others and may be very, very slow in accepting the "help" we wish to offer. Patience is a key. As one man whose wife suffers from chronic depression says, ''First you try everything you can think of to help . . . and nothing works. Next you try religious things . . . but they don't work, either. So then you wait. . . .'' Patience, gentleness, and most of all, sensitivity to the feelings of the depressed person are absolutely essential. It may be weeks or even months before he or she is ready to be ''helped.'' Even Jesus did not succeed in healing the blind man the first time.

PRAYER FOR HEALING OF PERCEPTION

Psalm 6

O Lord, do not condemn me in thy anger,
do not punish me in thy fury.

Be merciful to me, O Lord, for I am weak;
heal me, my very bones are shaken;

My soul quivers in dismay.
And thou, O Lord—how long?

Come back, O Lord; set my soul free,
deliver me for thy love's sake.

I am wearied with groaning;
all night long my pillow is wet with tears,
I soak my bed with weeping.

Grief dims my eyes;
they are worn out with all my woes.

The Lord has heard my entreaty;
the Lord will accept my prayer.

CHAPTER FOUR

DEPRESSION AND HOW WE THINK

Where do our thoughts come from? What makes us think as we do? "That's a silly question!" you say to yourself. "Our experiences and the things that happen to us make us think happy or depressed thoughts. What's so complicated about that?" Psychologists know, however, that it is not quite this simple.

In the previous chapter we noted how much expectations dictate the way we perceive ourselves and the world around us. These expectations are based on our *habits* or *patterns of thinking*. Our expectations help us to anticipate or to imagine what comes next: for example, in counting "1, 2, 3, _____" or "Mary had a little _____." Such expectations fill in the gaps by using memories of what we have experienced, learned and remembered earlier in life. An interesting inventory of expectations about oneself may be made by completing the statement "I am _____" twenty times. Some of your "I am _____" statements may describe you physically (e.g., tall), others in terms of your role, (e.g., a father), others your personality (e.g., sensitive), and so forth. Some people will think of themselves more often in terms of their role whereas others will characterize themselves more by their personality qualities. Such a descriptive and personal list gives us some hints about our own unique *self concept*.

The self concept is a composite of ideas, feelings and attitudes we have about ourselves. Just as our body grows and matures physically from the time of infancy, so also does our self concept. From the time of our childhood we have gradually learned how to protect our body and our self concept from injury or harm. Even if the self concept has developed in some unhealthy ways, we are so accustomed to these ways being part of ourselves that we strive to preserve them at all cost! Thus, patterns or habits of depressed thinking are often deeply ingrained in us. It seems perfectly normal for some people to think depressed thoughts because no contrary habit of thinking has become a part of their self concept. They are "at home" with these expected thoughts despite their unpleasant and painful consequences.

I (Dick) remember speaking with a university student who was failing his engineering courses. Each time he faced an examination in these subjects Tom was overwhelmed with thoughts of how inadequate he was for the task at hand. He seemed deeply convinced that he could not succeed. He felt miserable and anxious; he was unable to complete the examinations. He and I both knew that his negative self-appraisal of his academic ability was not accurate. He was in so many other ways a highly intelligent and competent person. My student friend recognized this but at the same time he was "at home" with his gnawing thoughts of inadequacy. No amount of persuasion could free him of this habit of thinking. As we prayed together an experience from his childhood came to mind. He recalled a time when at the age of ten he constructed a model plane from balsa wood. All went well until the tissue paper glued to the plane's wings was painted. The paint shrunk the tissue and the wings warped. The boy's father severely admonished him for his carelessness and for the many times during his childhood that he had failed to measure up to his parents' expectations. Later in his life Tom carried within his self concept the thought that he would never be able to please his father no matter how hard he tried. It was with this frame of mind that he approached his examinations.

Unhealthy or depressed thoughts which have become habitual are most resistant to change. Often no amount of chiding, convincing or reasoning will dislodge them. They have become an integral and protected part of one's self concept. Rather than asking Tom to make great efforts to disown his habit of thinking himself inadequate, I suggested that he visualize Jesus in the room with him during his childhood. I asked him to imagine once again the incident with the model plane and its warped wings. After some moments of silent prayer and imagination, he looked at me and smiled, ''You know what, Father?'' I encouraged him to share his obvious delight. ''It's remarkable! Jesus took the plane in his hands and studied it from many angles. He was really intrigued with it and asked me if he could keep it. He told me he had never had a plane like it!'' This incident, using imagination in prayer and welcoming God's healing, seemed to dislodge whatever was most resistant to change in the student's negative thinking. Examinations became less of an obstacle and today he is a successful engineer. Tom still battles the tendency to give in to negative thinking, but he also experiences the power of Christ's healing love in his life.

The human person is a very complex creature. Many of the processes of our inner lives are coordinated by our self concept and thus work together in harmony. To put it very simply, as human persons we have four very basic processes by which we stay in touch with our world. We perceive or sense—see, taste, smell, feel and hear. We think or reason—remember, imagine, hypothesize, conclude and solve problems. We feel or emote—love, hate, fear, feel guilty or depressed. We act or move—walk, play, eat, speak, etc. These four processes enable us to experience and to respond to the world around us.

Although each one of these processes is distinct in its own right, none occurs by itself. For instance, when you pick up a pen to sign your name to a check (you *act*), you see and touch the pen (you *perceive* what you are doing), you remember your name and imagine your handwriting (you *think* about it), and you may enjoy or dislike it. (You may have some *emotion* about making the payment).

When people complain of depression, some are most concerned about how they *feel* while others tell of how they have lost contact with their feelings. Some say they feel bad, sad, "down," or "blue." Others feel threatened by their inability to feel anything; they speak of lacking inner warmth or feelings. Feeling is a process which is intricately related to others—perceiving, thinking and acting.

We could picture it like this:

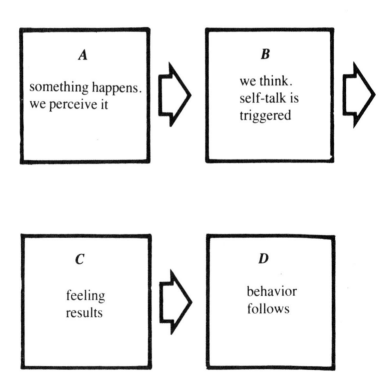

In this model, the experience of feeling depressed is only one event in a whole chain of events. It will be helpful for us to keep this sequence in mind.

Dr. Aaron Beck, a psychiatrist who has worked with many, many depressed patients, believes that the primary cause of depression is the habit of thinking incorrectly.[1] Because Dr. Beck's theory is considered to be one of the most important current theories of depression, it would be well worth our while to examine it carefully.

The process of thinking in such a fundamental function of human life that we ordinarily don't even notice it. We just *do* it. Seldom do we actually stop to think about *thinking*. Thinking can be described in several ways. We can call it "inner speech," "internal dialogue" (this is how the philosopher Plato referred to it), "self-talk," or any number of descriptive terms. Whatever we choose to label it, however, we are describing the fact that we think and remember with the aid of language which we articulate to ourselves. The way we perceive reality and consequently how we talk to ourselves about it is a vital key to unlocking the mystery of depression.

Characteristics of Depressed Thinking

Have you ever found yourself thinking thoughts such as these?
"I'm no good."
"I'm not attractive."
"I'm unworthy."
"I deserve to be depressed."
"I just can't."
"People will laugh at me."
"This will be a disaster."
"Things will never be any different."
"My friends think I'm stupid (ugly, boring, etc.)."

These are typical of the thought patterns which produce and maintain depression. The more depressed one is, the more such beliefs dominate one's thoughts. They are usually integrally connected to one's self concept and directly affect one's feelings and behavior. Other quick clues to such depression-producing self-talk are highly evaluative words like "should," "ought," or "must"; catastrophizing thoughts like "it's awful," "it's terrible," or "I just can't stand it"; and overgeneralizing such as "I'll never be able to do this" or "Nobody will ever like me."

Because he frequently misperceives and thus misinterprets the events of his daily life, the depressed person's thinking is often unrealistic. Above all, his thoughts are negative and self-defeating. Continuous unpleasant and unrealistic thoughts regarding one's self, one's experiences, and one's future are very typical of depression. Although the mental habits which have developed over many years and thus have become protected elements of one's self concept are stubbornly resistant to change, they can be overcome. The first step in changing these depression-fostering thought patterns is to learn to recognize them. For this reason we will examine the key characteristics of depressed thinking in more detail.

Depressed thinking is an insidious destroyer of self-confidence and good feelings. This is partly because negative thoughts tend to be *automatic*. In other words, we don't have to work at thinking depressing thoughts because they just come into our minds without being invited. As a matter of fact, we are often unaware of the continual "self-talk" that is going on inside our heads. The reason for this is that negative thinking is a well-learned habit, unintentionally strengthened by years of practice.

The automatic, nagative and painful thoughts of depression are almost always *unreasonable*; they are *irrational*. Negative thoughts are not arrived at through logic. One major illogical habit is the error of drawing a conclusion when there is no evidence on which to base it, or the evidence is directly contrary to the conclusion. Recalling the sequence of Situation, Thought, Feeling and Behavior, let's look at a typical example from everyday life.

A. Situation: You work particularly hard on an assignment but the boss doesn't compliment you
B. Thought: He doesn't like my work and he's going to fire me.
C. Feeling: Depression.
D. Behavior: Criticize the boss to co-workers

The conclusion that you are going to get fired is irrational because there is no evidence to support it. In fact, it is not even logical to deduce that he is displeased. There are other conclusions which are more logical. The boss could have been distracted by more urgent matters, not feeling well, or perhaps was late for an appointment. None of these alternative thoughts would produce feelings of depression. How different this brief interaction now appears! When we believe we know what others are thinking without asking, we are making an arbitrary inference, an irrational habit which can lead to depression.

Overgeneralization is a thinking error in which one assumes that a single experience is enough to tell how things always were and always will be. For example:

A. Situation: You lose a tennis match.
B. Thought: I'm no good at anything.
C. Feeling: Depression
D. Behavior: You give up tennis.

The loss of a single tennis game hardly demonstrates that one is even a bad tennis player, much less prove that one is a worthless and untalented person! This may seem like a trivial or even an unrealistic example, but most of our overgeneralizing conclusions which keep us depressed are just this silly when they are examined logically. Depression, of course, sometimes follows serious situations, problems, and life crises, but more often it is the result of habitually misperceiving and illogically responding to the innumerable "small" interactions and events of everyday life. Over-generalizations and negative thoughts reinforce a negative self concept, keeping one depressed.

Another related irrational habit which can lead to depression is to ignore the positive and accentuate the negative. We often over-emphasize our failures and minimize our successes. A father becomes depressed when his son, for whom he had such high hopes, drops out of school. The present difficulty, he concludes, proves that he is a total failure as a parent. He is unable to find consolation in recalling the many satisfying moments with his son and the wisdom which he has successfully applied to family problems in the past. Many of the responses a parent makes to his children are neither 100% "wrong" nor 100% "right"; usually they reflect both love and frustration, wisdom and impatience. Instead of recognizing this, however, this loving and concerned father depresses himself by criticizing his parenting and himself as a failure. This is an example of both overgeneralization and accentuating the negative/minimizing the positive. When we put labels on ourselves (like stupid, failure, bore, etc.) we are usually overgeneralizing and accentuating the negative.

Magnification or catastrophizing is the irrational, depressing habit of exaggerating. Events are seen in an extreme way. For example:

A. Situation: Your fiance is killed in a plane crash.
B. Thought: I can't go on without him/her.
C. Feeling: Deep depression
D. Behavior: Attempted suicide

In this kind of thinking, the significance of a perhaps genuinely stressful event is blown out of proportion. At the same time that the event is magnified, one's ability to cope with it is minimized. Magnification is the negative thought process which causes one to believe that normal feelings of sadness, hurt or grief will never pass. Thoughts that begin "I can't" should be immediately suspected as possible cases of magnification.

When we take time to carefully examine and identify our self-talk, then, we discover that it almost always reflects a false, distorted view of reality. The negative things we tell ourselves range from mild distortions to complete misrepresentations. We jump to conclusions that are completely false. Although we do not consciously mean to exaggerate or make over-generalizations, these are common in our self-talk. Our automatic negative thinking, because it is so inaccurate, serves absolutely no useful purpose and almost always makes us feel worse.

Depressed thinking, because it has been such a life-long habit, has a tendency to appear perfectly normal, no matter how unrealistic and unreasonable it is. This is why it has such a powerful effect over us. We believe our negative thoughts without questioning them. Just because we think something, however, does not make it true. Since many of our thoughts are so repetitive (''I'm no good,'' ''I can't succeed,'' ''No one will ever love me''), we accept them wholeheartedly simply because we have been thinking them so often and for so many years. We irrationally believe these familiar thoughts, which form our self concept, to be facts. The more we believe them, though, the more damaging and depressing they are.

The Triad of Depression

Negative thoughts generally fall into three categories. These are negative notions about self, the world (events in our lives and our relationships with others), and the future. Together these are what Dr. Beck[2] calls the ''Triad of Depression'':

SELF
(helpless)

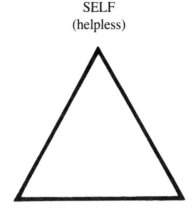

THE FUTURE   THE WORLD
(no hope)   (impossible obstacles)

The Triad of Depression

Thoughts About Self

Depression is very "I-centered." By this we do not mean self-centered in the same sense as "selfish." Rather, depression creates a frame of mind in which almost everything one experiences is a reminder of one's own miserable, helpless condition. This is partly why depression is so painful: not because the individual believes others have let him down but because he believes himself to be to blame for his own predicament. Every experience is filtered through an "I-filter."

Depressed people wrongly hold themselves responsible for so much that happens in the world around them. For example, a depressed mother blames herself for her children's sicknesses; a baseball player feels it is all his fault that his team lost the game. Not only are failures emphasized and magnified, but successes are ignored or brushed aside as accidental. Depressed people often anchor their sense of self-worth to a very narrow idea of what constitutes success. Unrealistic expectations and impossibly high goals inevitably lead to an overwhelming sense of failure and worthlessness. In other words, the depressed person sets himself up to fail.

The mental habit of inflating others and deflating oneself is also typical of depression. The effect of these comparisons is to distort perception of others who are incorrectly perceived as perfect paragons of talent and virtue. In contrast, the negative perception of oneself leads to the false conclusion that one is hopelessly inferior—stupid, unattractive, untalented and unspiritual. Whenever a depressed person uses his imaginary measuring stick to see how he measures up to others, he inevitably comes out the loser.

Unrealistic comparisons lead one right into unrealistic notions of what one should or should not be. Often these notions have their origins in the unrealistic expectations which are sometimes unwittingly imposed upon us by others, the church, and society in general. These beliefs and self-statements, easily recognized because they usually begin ''I should,'' are common among depressed people:

> ''I should never say no to people if I want them to like me.''
> ''I should pray at least on hour a day if I'm a good Christian.''
> ''I should have a deep, rich inner life.''
> ''I should always enjoy playing with my children.''
> ''I should be more cheerful and more out-going.''
> ''I shouldn't have these sexual feelings.''
> ''I should be more considerate of others.''

These ''shoulds'' are so incorporated into one's thinking that they become one's own private and unrealistic rules for living. A depressed person wrote about these ''should'' rules:

> As is so often the case lately, there are many ''shoulds'' and ''should nots'' echoing through my head. ''Christians should entrust their cares to God.'' ''Christians shouldn't worry.''

"Christians should be peaceful, joyful, happy, secure, content. . . ." What does God call me to be? The *real* me, the *should* me, or the me I *want* to be?

"Shoulds," "musts," and "oughts" can so dominate one's thinking that when they are not obeyed or fulfilled in one's life they produce depression and an agonizing sense of failure. The "shoulds" create a constant inner tension between one's heart's desire and one's situation or circumstances in life. The greater the distance between the desires of one's heart and one's circumstances, the greater the feeling of loneliness and depression.

This "tyranny of the shoulds" is not the same thing as having norms for behavior of reasonable goals for oneself. Certainly the establishment of realistic goals and standards is a positive and growth-enhancing practice. The difference between such healthy notions and depression-producing ones is the degree to which they are realistic. Depresssed persons often *over*apply rules regarding what they should do or be, thus they program themselves for failure. Living with tyrannical "shoulds" leaves one feeling helpless and worthless.

Thoughts About Others and the World

The second angle of Beck's Triad of Depression is built from negative thoughts about others and the world. Largely based on distorted perceptions, the person who is depressed misconstrues his experiences. When confronted with a job to be done, he tells himself, "It's way beyond my abilities. I can never do it." Rigid thinking keeps one from trying new things. Thus when one solution does not work out, the depressed individual prematurely concludes that there are no others. Depression works in this way to keep him chained to his unhappy lot in life. Negative thinking encourages this passivity and helplessness.

The "I-centeredness" typical in depression produces a painful self-consciousness. Because the depressed person is preoccupied thinking that he is stupid, unattractive, boring and sinful, he mistakenly believes that others are observing him and noting his inadequacies. What others say and do is easily misinterpreted as rejection. Depression always leads one to believe the worst.

Thoughts About the Future

Negative beliefs about the future make up the third angle of the Triad. It is easy to believe that things will never change. Severe feelings of depression are all-engrossing. The abject discouragement which makes one feel so miserable seemingly occupies every nook and cranny. Depression affects us physically, mentally and spiritually. It touches not only the present but is intimately tied to our past and the future as well. As we said in the second chapter, being seriously depressed is like living in a dark pit. The pit is a very deep one, so deep that one cannot see over the sides at life outside. All that one is aware of is darkness, silence, personal isolation, and the terrifying feeling that this imprisoned life will never improve.

The hopelessness for the future has its roots in a distorted view of the past. Hurts, failures, and embarassments are magnified in one's memory. These exaggerated memories now seem to be a prediction of the future. The faulty thinking of depression leads one to conclude that if something was true in the past then it is always true. Such illogical thinking immortalizes bad experiences, failure and rejection, and effectively sabotages present attempts at growth and happiness.

Negative beliefs and self-statements are emotionally distressing—they make us feel discouraged. They also significantly increase the likelihood that failure or rejection actually will result, making us even more depressed than ever. When we believe these negative things about ourselves we are less likely to do our best. Then if we actually do fail, we say "I told you so" and are more convinced than ever that we are stupid, unlovable, and unsuccessful. We could look at this vicious circle this way:

SYMPTOMS OF DEPRESSION

(such as: sadness, guilt, crying, in
decisiveness, withdrawal, insomnia,
chronic tiredness, etc.)

**BELIEFS ABOUT SELF, THE
WORLD AND THE FUTURE**

(such as: "I'll never feel better, "I'm
just no good," "I'm a terrible wife and
mother," "I must be losing my mind,"
"God has abandoned me," etc.)

The more negative beliefs we have, the more we feel depressed. In
turn, the more depressed we become—feeling "down," physically tired, withdrawing from others, decreasing our activity,
etc.—the more depressing thoughts we have. It is a downward
spiral from which there seems to be no escape.

Fundamental Beliefs and Depression

We have been examining some very common maladaptive
thinking habits. Jumping to conclusions, assuming we know what
others are thinking, ignoring the positive while accentuating the
negative, and exaggeration are all examples of bad habits which
play a large role in creating and sustaining depression. In addition
to these faulty thought patterns, however, depressed individuals
cling to a fundamentally irrational philosophy of life. Underlying
our feelings and behavior are a number of general beliefs about life.
These beliefs, which we will examine shortly, are so deeply im-

planted in our approach to life that we are usually not even aware of them. Unconscious or not, however, these beliefs serve as filters which subtly color and distort our view of self, the world and the future.

A number of psychologists, most notably Dr. Albert Ellis, have been concerned about these fundamental beliefs and the effect they have on our feelings and behavior. Dr. Ellis is a psychotherapist and a pioneer in the relatively new field of cognitive restructuring (i.e., therapy which is aimed at changing thinking patterns). Rational-Emotive Therapy, sometimes referred to simply as RET, is an approach designed by Dr. Ellis to deal with a wide variety of emotional problems. One of the major unique features of RET is the conviction that certain core irrational ideas are at the root of most emotional disturbances. Once they are identified, these basic ideas and attitudes, just like the negative self-talk which they spawn, can be unlearned, according to Ellis, Beck, and other cognitive psychologists.

Just what are the irrational ideas which people so often believe to be true? Of course, there are as many variations of these beliefs as there are people to believe in them, but the following are the major irrational ideas which Dr. Ellis identified.[3]

1. It is a dire necessity to be loved or approved by virtually every significant other person in the community.
2. One should be thoroughly competent, adequate, and achieving in all possible respects if one is to consider oneself worthwhile.
3. Certain people are bad, wicked or villainous and should be severely blamed and punished.
4. It is awful and catastrophic when things are not the way one would very much like them to be.
5. Human unhappiness is externally caused and people have little or no ability to control their sorrows and disturbances.
6. If something is or may be dangerous or fearsome one

should be terribly concerned about it and should keep dwelling on the possibility of its occurring.

7. It is easier to avoid than to face certain life difficulties and self-responsibilities.

8. One should be dependent on others and one needs someone stronger than oneself on whom to rely.

9. One's past history is an all-important determiner of one's present behavior and because something once strongly affected one's life, it should indefinitely have a similar effect.

10. One should become quite upset over other people's problems and disturbances.

11. There is invariably a right, precise and perfect solution to human problems and it is catastrophic if this perfect solution is not found.

The research of Drs. K.A. LaPointe and C.J. Crandall[4] has revealed that depressed people are particularly bothered by Irrational Ideas 2, 4, 5, 7 and 8. This specific set of beliefs provides a rough profile of depression: high self-expectations (this is the most commonly-held belief among depressed people), over-reaction to frustration, a tendency to not accept responsibility for one's life, problem avoidance, and dependency. Of course, we probably do not think in just these same words. It is, however, very likely that each of us unconsciously holds one or more of these beliefs. Though we know it or not, such irrational thinking has a persistent effect on how we experience life, how we feel, and thus how we behave. These irrational notions create a philosophy of living which is self-defeating and unhealthy.

By holding to these or similar beliefs we make ourselves depressed and frustrated. As Dr. Ellis says, "Neurosis essentially seems to consist of stupid behavior by a non-stupid person."[5] No one deliberately makes himself feel depressed. Yet we all do things which have precisely this result. Why? Largely because of ignorance and well-established habit. Unfortunately, these attitudes are often instilled at an early age by parents, church, and the mass media of our modern-day society. These thoughts/beliefs became automatic when we were children and, as we have said, we are more or less unaware of their presence and influence. They have become incorporated into our self concept. It is important to think through these irrational ideas carefully, to challenge them, and to replace them with rational, healthy beliefs.

Thinking Realistically

Rational thinking is not the same as "positive" thinking. It is very important to make this distinction. Rational thinking is *realistic* thinking. It is just as irrational to tell yourself that things are going along just fine when all your friends are avoiding you as it is to conclude that you are therefore a totally unattractive, worthless person and that this is a terrible, awful situation. The realistic—thus rational—response to such an occurrence would be to face up to the objective evidence that this signifies a problem in relating to others. Only then can efforts be made to remedy the situation.

Rational thinking is an essential element of learning to abide in the truth. Although we would dearly like to believe so, there is no easy, sure-fire formula for living happily ever after. We do not live in a fairytale world but in a real one in which things will not always go our way. We will without a doubt experience disappointments, rejections and failures. We will make unwise choices; we will sin. Even though we work at countering our irrational beliefs and negative self-talk, we may still legitimately feel sad, regretful and unhappy. As a matter of fact, there are situations in which it would be inappropriate *not* to feel sad.

When we abide in the truth we are willing to accept the fact when we are wrong or have behaved badly. This realistic, honest and rational appraisal is healthy and leads to growth. How different this is from the self-hate and self-condemnation of depression! By becoming more and more aware of our self-talk and underlying beliefs we will learn to discriminate between rational and irrational thinking. When we are firmly rooted in reality we will then be able to make appropriate responses. Healthy thinking habits lead to appropriate feelings, which in turn stimulate responsible and mature behavior.

Footnotes

1. Aaron T. Beck et al., *Cognitive Therapy of Depression* (New York: The Guilford Press, 1979), p. 19.
2. Beck et al., p. 11.
3. Albert Ellis and Robert A. Harper, *A New Guide to Rational Living* (No. Hollywood, Calif.: Wilshire Book Co., 1977), pp. 198-200.
4. K.A. LaPointe and C.J. Crandall, ''Relationship of Irrational Beliefs to Self Reported Depression,'' Unpublished manuscript.
5. Ellis and Harper, p. 37.

A SCRIPTURAL MEDITATION ON THINKING

Seek the Lord while he may be found, call him while he is near. Let the scoundrel forsake his way, and the wicked man his thoughts. For my thoughts are not your thoughts, nor are your ways my ways, says the Lord. As high as the heavens are above the earth, so high are my ways above your ways and my thoughts above your thoughts (Is 55:6-9).

How deep are the riches and the wisdom and the judgment of God! How inscrutable his judgments, how unsearchable his ways! For ''who has known the mind of the Lord? Or who has been his counselor?'' And now, brothers, do not conform yourselves to this age, but be transformed by the renewal of your mind, so that you may judge what is God's will, what is good, pleasing and perfect (Rm 11:33-34, 12:1-2).

You must lay aside your former way of life and the old self which deteriorates through illusion and desire, and acquire a fresh, spiritual way of thinking. You must put on that new man created in God's image, whose justice and holiness are born of truth (Ep 4:22-23).

May the God of our Lord Jesus Christ, the Father of glory, grant you a spirit of wisdom and insight to know him clearly. May he enlighten your innermost vision that you may know the great hope to which he has called you, the wealth of his glorious heritage to be distributed among the members of the church, and the immeasurable scope of his power in us who believe (Ep 1:17-19).

CHAPTER FIVE

DEPRESSION AND ACTIVITY

There are many ways to look at the problem of depression and just as many ways to treat it. Professionals who work in the area of mental health are continually searching for more effective approaches to this common but complicated problem. At a recent international annual meeting of the Society for Psychotherapy Research in Oxford, England, it was noted that among the many forms of treatment, cognitive-behavioral therapy for depression is clearly one of the most effective mental health therapies today.

An active, "let's deal with the here-and-now" approach, cognitive-behavioral therapy is not concerned with what may have happened back in one's childhood. Instead, behavior therapists encourage their clients to respond to the situations and relationships in their day-to-day world. This active and "now-oriented" approach may come as a bit of a surprise to you. For a long time psychology has been concerned with carefully analyzing the events of one's past life, working to search out those traumatic or hurtful experiences which were believed to be responsible for one's fears, anxieties and depression. According to these traditional psychologies (known as "psychodynamic" theories), healing will come when one is able to achieve insight into these past hurts. This healing insight usually is the result of a lengthy process of "talking through" one's problems. Behavior therapy, on the other hand, is not a "talking cure" but an energetic approach to the learning of new ways of thinking, acting, and feeling.

When speaking of an active, "now-oriented" approach to life, I (Dick) recall a recent delightful conversation with a lively seventy year old woman named Laura. She was enroute to visit her relatives in Germany. During the flight from the West Coast to Chicago, she told me of her lifelong experiences with depression, especially during the past few months since her husband's death after a long terminal illness. Laura deeply grieved his death and keenly felt her loss. "I guess you realize how hard it is for a devoted married person to become a widow or widower after so many years of close companionship. . . . But, I am doing quite well these days. Despite my bouts with sadness, I'm not letting myself get mired down. I keep my mind active and manage to get out of the house every day. In fact, that's why I'm making this adventure over to Germany on the spur of the moment. I decided it would do me good to get away from home for awhile."

Laura told me of how during these past months she had been helping another widow in her neighborhood who was depressed and not caring for herself adequately. She made it her concern each day to take and share a balanced meal with this neighbor. Laura confided that she gained a new friend during those months but, most of all, she gained much satisfaction in seeing this friend regain both her interest in people and improved physical, emotional and spiritual health. Laura had learned and was using a very effective strategy for dealing with her own depression.

A Bit of Theory

As we saw in the last chapter, practically everything that we do is related to what we have learned. As a matter of fact, the ways we walk, talk, play, think, believe and feel are all learned and become our self concept. In the process of living with our world and with other people, we learn to draw certain conclusions about our experiences. Our memories of our life experiences are, in turn, constantly used with evey new set of circumstances and thus strongly influence our actions (behavior) in any situation. In this way our human abilities to sense, perceive, think, remember, feel and choose are all related to learning and behavior. Let's look briefly now at some basic principles of psychology that concern learning and behavior.

To put it very simply, one way that we learn is by making an association or connection in our memory between our experiences and our feelings. For example:

> Because she feels awkward and shy, Susan is very ill at ease in social situations. She soon learns to spare herself this tension by avoiding people and isolating herself. Susan has learned to withdraw from life in order to cope.

> John takes a hard, critical look at his life and concludes he's a failure as a Christian. Miserable, he starts missing church and avoiding his Christian friends. Before long he feels even more guilty than before and is sure God cannot possibly love him now.

> Andrea is very lonely, and finds that when she talks with others about her health problems they demonstrate much love and concern. Eventually Andrea learns to think of herself as "sick" and is always looking for someone who can talk with her about her troubles.

In each of these examples behaviors and the feelings that go with them are learned because the individual associates what he or she does or fails to do with certain consequences.

An essential element in learning is what psychologists call *reinforcement*. Reinforcement is any event that increases the likelihood or probability of an action or response. We will continue to act or not act in a given way if our behavior wins us pleasurable positive rewards or if it leads to the removal of unpleasant consequences from our lives. By way of illustration, Laura experiences much happiness in seeing her depressed neighbor brighten with new interest and health. Her efforts to help were positively re-

warded by a sense of accomplishment and by a growing companionship with this new friend. At the same time, some of the
unpleasant consequences of her own personal sadness were lifted
as she actively reached out to another in need.

Laura was fortunate to experience in a relatively short time
such positive outcomes both in her own situation and in her neighbor's life. Helping people afflicted with depression or being helped
by another when suffering emotional pain is most often without
immediate rewards. Such helping or being helped often requires
heroic patience and trust. Laura is one of these people who has
learned this during her life. She also learned through the months of
her husband's terminal illness the *art* of helping others.

Usually we continue to act in ways which bring pleasurable
results or feelings but we will stop acting in a manner which leads
to undesirable consequences. As we shall see, however, our actions sometimes have more than one outcome. The immediate
consequence may be pleasurable and thus it serves to reinforce the

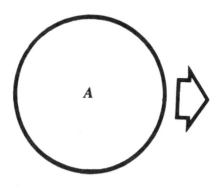

Antecedent events,
thoughts and feelings

action. The long-term, delayed consequences, on the other hand, may be very negative and undesirable. An example of such dual consequences is the habit of eating candy bars. The eating of sugar-laden candy is immediately and strongly reinforced by the pleasure of the good taste of the candy and by the surge of energy which results from increased blood sugar. On the other hand, the eating of candy has other consequences which are not at all desirable. These include hours in the dentist's chair and additional pounds of weight. (Many people also find that the intake of refined sugars in candy and other sweets produces a burst of energy which is followed by a "low"). This simple example helps to illustrate one reason why we often act in unreasonable ways. As human beings we unfortunately seem to learn some unhealthy, self-defeating habits just as easily as we learn behaviors which enhance our growth and happiness.

We can briefly picture the learning sequence with this very simple diagram:

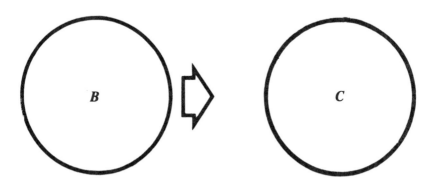

Behavior or
Actions

Consequences, including
feelings about A & B

There are three very basis elements of the learning sequence as we have pictured it here: prior or antecedent experiences, thoughts, and feelings (A); the behavior itself (B); and the consequences of the behavior (C).

Antecedents are all of the important elements of the situation which come *before* the behavior. There may be one significant antecedent or many. An antecedent can be any one of a variety of things: a person, place, thought, time of day, physical condition, or event which stimulates behavior. The sight of and thoughts about Laura's neighbor friend and her needs are *antecedents*.

Behavior is something you *do*; it does not include what you think, decide, wish, remember or feel. Taking food down to a neighbor and sharing a meal are examples of *behavior*.

Consequences are the events or feelings that follow behavior. Consequences that give pleasure are rewards and those which are unpleasant are punishments. Consequences may also be neutral. As we have seen, the consequences are very important because of their power to reinforce or extinguish behavior. The *consequences* of Laura's behavior are her friend's improved health and her own inner happiness and self-satisfaction.

To help us see the learning process more clearly we can analyze our earlier examples like this:

Antecedent	Behavior	Consequences	Learning
Susan's shyness and lack of social skills	Susan avoids social situations and contact with people	Immediate: decreased tension Long-term: aloneness	"I can avoid tension by avoiding people"
John's mistaken views of sin, self & God	John shuts out God and the Christian community because he feels unworthy	The joy John once knew evaporates & he is even more convinced that he is unworthy of God's love	"I'm no good. God can't possibly love me."

Andrea's lone- liness	Looking for re- lief, Andrea seeks out others to whom she can talk about her problems	Others respond with concern & attention and Andrea feels loved and cared for	"People love me when I'm 'sick.'"

As we look at these examples we begin to see something of a pattern. Susan, John and Andrea are all people who are hurting and who are struggling in perhaps the only ways they know how to find solutions for the unhappiness in their lives. When we analyze their decisions which are not intentionally unhealthy and the consequences which result from them, it becomes apparent that sometimes one's attempts to cope only bring a greater sense of loneliness, failure and depression. Perhaps, then, it would be a bit more accurate to draw our learning sequence like this:

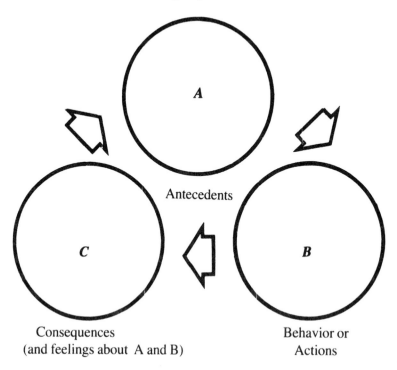

A

Antecedents

C

B

Consequences
(and feelings about A and B)

Behavior or
Actions

Now we have a vicious circle. The consequences (sometimes referred to as "pay-offs") reinforce our behavior and lock us into a self-sabotaging game which guarantees that we will become and remain losers. Although we are almost never consciously aware of what is occurring, we *learn* to keep ourselves depressed by unintentionally falling into unhealthy patterns or habits of thinking.

One vicious circle so characteristic of depression looks like this:

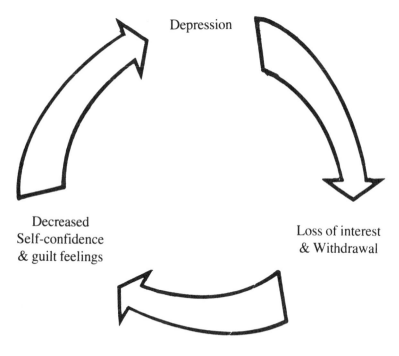

Depression

Decreased
Self-confidence
& guilt feelings

Loss of interest
& Withdrawal

The beginning and the end melt together and it is difficult to sort out which comes first. Depression with its physical and emotional symptoms almost always creates a strong urge to withdraw. But when we withdraw hoping to find some relief from our discomfort, we find that our withdrawal has only created a greater sense of guilt and remorse. The *antecedents* of depression (failure, loss, stress, lack of social skills, etc.) produce the characteristic *behavior* of depression (withdrawal, talking about one's troubles, a tendency to neglect one's health, inactivity, etc.). These behaviors have inevitable *consequences* such as feelings of helplessness and emptiness, not caring, physical fatigue, alienation from friends and family, loneliness, etc. The depression suffered by Laura's friend "pulled" her into isolation, away from healthy relationships with others. Overwhelmed with a sense of worthlessness, she neglected to eat regularly. Such a lack of care only fortified her depression making life all the more unbearable. Caught in this vicious circle, one feels oneself spiraling down, down, down into the dark and seemingly bottomless pit of depression.

A Learning Approach to Depression

How, you may ask, is all of this related to the healing of depression? How was Laura able to manage her own depression so effectively? She managed it in several significant ways, as you may have already guessed. Dr. Peter M. Lewinsohn, and his colleagues at the University of Oregon, have developed a theory of depression and a method of treatment that are directly related to learning.

Like all behavioral psychologists, Dr. Lewinsohn[1] is concerned with *current* events and does not look for the causes of present problems (like depression) in past events (such as being rejected early in life, etc.). Rather, he believes that we think, feel and behave as we do because of the reinforcements we are receiving *now* from our environment and from ourselves. Thus we could say that *depression is a set of behaviors and feelings that are reinforced by pleasant and unpleasant life experiences.* In this sense, we could say that many aspects of depression are unintentionally learned and have become strong habits.

According to learning theory, behavior that is not reinforced will not continue but will be extinguished eventually, that is, it will stop. Depression—like any other set of behaviors, both healthy and unhealthy—is being regularly protected in our self concept by some source of reinforcement. Look at your own behavior: what is the "pay-off" (reinforcement) that supports it? What are the antecedents to depressive behavior? What are the consequences? We need to discover the factors of "pay-offs" in our lives which are maintaining our depression so that they can be changed and the depression controlled or relieved.

If we continue to live our lives in ways which bring us negative consequences we will become or stay depressed. Similarly, when we make no successful efforts to enjoy positive pay-offs or consequences, we become or stay depressed. It is the balance between the two which is important. More often than not, the problem is not what we *do* but what we *don't* do. In other words, it is not so much a matter of living in ways which produce depressed feelings as it is that we become depressed because we are *not* doing those things which bring us the very vital feelings of confidence, self-worth, peacefulness and joy.

What factors in a person's life make him more vulnerable to depression? The cycle of depression *begins* for many people because of certain factors:

1. Difficulty With Friendship and Social Situations

The depression-prone person often finds it very hard to relate with others. At times one's own overwhelming feelings of loneliness and sadness magnify awkwardness into inability to communicate with another. At other times depressed people experience such an inner emptiness that it seems virtually impossible to relate or to share anything having to do with one's own emotions and feelings. Being ill at ease with others may grow into acute discomfort in social situations and friendship. This is both exasperating and depressing. As a result, the depressed person is tempted to avoid social situations and to withdraw from friendships. As this happens one becomes even more caught up in guilt. The vicious circle may be broken by making small, gradual efforts to counteract this withdrawal by going out to others and by taking more initiative in friendship. At times these efforts will feel "heroic," but with much patience they will begin to reap positive results.

2. *Unfortunate or Devastating Life Circumstances*

Any number of personal misfortunes may trigger an episode of depression for the depression-prone person. Depressed people are especially susceptible to the stresses of financial worry, sickness or poor health, social isolation, and lack of employment opportunity. More severe stress from loss and separation resulting from rejection, divorce or death makes one especially vulnerable to depression. Feelings of inability to cope with stressful or tragic events, whether anticipated or unexpected, fuel depression all the more. One may fall deeper into helplessness and a sense of being abandoned. Simply knowing there is no way to restore what was broken or lost from our lives seems of no avail. The decision to do some adventuring or something enjoyable for oneself may often help to break this vicious cycle. Such acts of kindness to oneself must be repeated if they are to overcome the withdrawal tendencies associated with depression.

3. *Failures With One's Children, Marriage or Job*

The experience and reality of failure may leave one with the notion that he's a hopeless loser. Depression-prone parents, who view their children's success as an extension of their own goodness, can be devastated when their children's lives do not meet with parental expectations. For one or many painful and unfortunate reasons a marriage or job can end. These difficult experiences are deeply sensed as personal failures and, for the depressed person, involve much self-incrimination. Failures especially confirm for the depressed person what he has always been saying to himself: "I am no good."

Our success and image-oriented society certainly does not reward failures. Perhaps rather than being overwhelmed by striving to make oneself and others conform to false values of success and attractiveness, one might try, with the help of a friend or counselor, to affirm and to express one's abilities and good qualities. This gradual process of locating and *expressing* one's abilities and goodness is suggested to counteract "I am no good" thinking and behavior.

These three factors—lack of friendship and social skills, life circumstances, and failure experiences, are *antecedents* which lead to the depressive *behaviors* of passivity and withdrawal. Together they produce the inevitable *consequences* of negative reinforcement—overwhelming feelings of discouragement, disheartenment and weakness.

Why do depressed people find it so difficult to relate to others and to muster any more energy?

There are many possible reasons, of course, but frequently it is because one is not alert to the fact that one's lifestyle is simply not providing enough opportunities for one to feel good about oneself. For example, Laura had and acted upon a deep conviction that her trip to Germany would help her immensely. We all need fun times; we need to do things that lift our attention off our problems, and for this to happen we need to get out of the rut we are in. The purpose for emphasizing this is to suggest that you can *do* something about depressed feelings. These behavior patterns are so deeply imbedded in our self concept that, even when discovered, they are very difficult to change. We are most resistant to leaving a way which we know—even if it is a rut—for new uncharted, untravelled paths. As irrational as it may sound, sometimes we clutch onto our familiar misery rather than change to the uncertainty of a new way of living. It takes a courageous "leap of hope" for most of us to make real and lasting changes in our lifestyles.

The first step toward greater freedom from depression is to *recognize* what is happening in one's life that is feeding depressive feelings and behavior. Once you have identified your own unique depression cycles, you can then begin doing something to remedy the situation and thus your depression-proneness. Sometimes we become aware of this when we are doing new activities or getting to know new people.

A key area to investigate when looking for the depression-producers in one's life is the vital area of human relationships. God created us to need each other. Sometimes we lose track of this truth and try to go it alone. There seems to be something inside each of us which yearns for independence and total self-reliance. We fool ourselves into believing that to be a "rugged individualist" is to be free. Or we may tell ourselves that children need others but grown-ups do not. Sometimes in our attempts to please others we deny our true feelings and our deep inner pain, thinking that by "keeping a stiff upper lip" we can hide our deepest needs. The result of mistaken ideas like these is a life that is strangled by its own supposed strength: a lifestyle that breeds loneliness and depression.

Being alone is not always the life of choice. Sometimes an unwelcome aloneness is brought about by death or separation from a loved one, by divorce, or by rejection. These things do happen and they inevitably bring sadness and mourning. The people we love the most have the greatest power over us. Their love and presence bring us joy and make us feel whole and worthwhile. When something intervenes and disrupts these kinds of essential relationships, we lose very important sources of reinforcement.

Naturally we all have many relationships in our lives which involve varying degrees of attachment and affection. Beyond our immediate circle of close friends we have an ever-broadening group of co-workers, neighbors and acquaintances. These, too, are important. Every encounter with others holds within it the potential for the giving and receiving of respect, affection and approval. Very often this is done without even speaking a word. When, because of shyness, fear, or life circumstances we are deprived of this vital closeness, we are impoverished. We need the indispensable reinforcement that comes from human relationships.

The combination of outer adversities and inner depression

often creates an overwhelming feeling of inertia. It is as though every ounce of energy has been drained off, making it very, very hard to reach out to others just when we need to do this the most. One feels overcome by a terrible, paralyzing lethargy.

Although most depressed people complain of a chronic energy shortage with its attendant tiredness, withdrawal, and "don't care" attitude, some individuals react in an opposite fashion. These are "workaholics," persons who strive to immerse themselves in continual activity, whether it be work, sports, ministry, social events or hobbies. These people are also more susceptible to getting caught up in addictions like excessive eating or drinking, drugs, compulsive gambling. By such immersion in positive and/or negative activities, they are warding off threatening feelings of inner emptiness or "blankness." It would be a mistake to assume, however, that such persons are knowingly working to escape their depression. On the contrary, the "Activity Syndrome" is usually an unconscious defense used by people who are not ordinarily aware of their depression.

There are times when the depressed person will be unable to ask others like Laura for help and will choose to rely on "self-help" strategies for healing, such as those described in Chapter IX.

The Strength in Remembering

In some ways the grief of losing a loved one becomes a natural self-help process. Years ago a mother of a large family of nine children was suddenly widowed following the death of her husband in a fatal accident. Through the years of her marriage she was the "heart" of their family life. The husband had cared for so many other details like taxes, license plates, and house repairs. As she recovered from the shock of his death she realized how many new demands faced her—things which had never entered her mind before.

She was sometimes overwhelmed by desperate feelings of helplessness. But she continued to keep her family and home together. During the months and years following her husband's death she would think of him, of their conversations together, of how he did things for the family. Gradually she acquired the mind and ability to function in many new ways. It was as if during her grief she gained for herself and the children some of what was lost from their family. Today she is one of those very wise, honored widows to whom many people come for counsel and wisdom.

At the Last Supper Jesus spoke of his impending death. The apostles and friends must have been filled with fear, wondering how they would be able to carry on without him. He assured them they would not be left orphans in the world. Consider his words (Jn 16:20-22; 15:26-27; 14:26, 12-14):

> In very truth I tell you, you will weep and mourn. . . . But though you will be plunged in grief, your grief will be turned to joy. A woman in labor is in pain because her time has come; but when the child is born she forgets the anguish in her joy that a man has been born into the world. So it is with you: for the moment you are sad at heart; but I shall see you again, and then you will be joyful, and no one shall rob you of your joy.
>
> But when your Advocate has come, whom I will send you from the Father—the Spirit of truth that issues from the Father—he will bear witness to me. And you also are my witnesses, because you have been with me from the first.
>
> Your Advocate, the Holy Spirit whom the Father will send in my name, will teach you everything, and will call to mind all that I have told you.
>
> In truth, in very truth I tell you, he who has faith in me will do what I am doing; and he will do greater things still because I am going to the Father. Indeed anything you ask in my name I will do, so that the Father may be glorified in the Son. If you ask anything in my name I will do it.

Jesus promises to send his Spirit to abide in our hearts, lives and families. He told us that the Spirit would bring to our minds the *words* of Jesus and the *life* he lived. As we become more familiar with the life and words of Christ, like the widow who remembered her husband and became strong for others, we are blessed with a new strength and understanding. This gift of the Spirit of Jesus is available to each of us for the asking.

Footnotes

1. P.M. Lewinsohn, "A Behavioral Approach to Depression," in *The Psychology of Depression: Contemporary Theory and Research*, ed. R.J. Friedman and M.M. Katz (Washington, D.C.: Winston/Wiley, 1974).

CHAPTER SIX

DEPRESSION AND THE SPIRITUAL LIFE

My God, my God, why have you forsaken me,
Far from my prayer, from the words of my cry?
O my God, I cry out by day, and you answer not;
By night, and there is no relief for me (Ps 22:2-3).

Depression is not only a physical and emotional problem, but it is a spiritual problem as well. In fact, for the individual who is concerned with spiritual matters, the impact of depression on one's spiritual life is keenly felt. Our thoughts and emotions continually influence that part of us which we call our spirit. Because of this very close relationship, a disturbance in one affects the other. It is important to recognize this for it helps to understand why we also experience the effects of depression in our spiritual life.

The best way to describe the spiritual experience of depression is to think of it in terms of darkness. This comparison seems apt, because darkness is the opposite of all that we think of as resulting from the light of God in our lives. In other words, when we are depressed we feel unhappy and discontented instead of joyful and peaceful; we feel barren and empty instead of filled with the Spirit; we are overcome with doubts and despair instead of faith and hope; we feel guilty, sinful and unworthy instead of redeemed, forgiven, cherished and loved by the Father; lastly, we feel abandoned and alone, cut off from the light and life-giving presence of God. This *darkness* seems to cast us deeper into depression than ever.

The reader may recognize the fact that these spiritual "symptoms" may be related to other phenomena besides depression. For example, God may be leading one into a deeper way of prayer, faith and union with himself. Such purifying spiritual changes may even bring an end to one's cherished and consoling experiences in prayer. As one is led to follow Christ more by faith than by feelings, a sense of abandonment, spiritual dryness, or a "desert experience" is not uncommon. Because of this possibility, there is no good substitute for discernment. When a Christian experiences spiritual darkness like this for any prolonged period, it would be advisable to seek discernment and counsel from an experienced spiritual director or pastoral advisor in order to determine the source of the problem.

In this chapter we will examine some of the effects depression has on the spiritual life, such as the darkness of guilt feelings, the darkness of doubt, and the darkness of emptiness. We will then explore some ways of dealing with darkness, and some common responses will be described and evaluated. The special problem of prayer in darkness will be explored, and lastly, we will look at the question of the cross and what it means in our lives.

The Darkness of Guilt Feelings

There is nothing like depression for making one feel shut off from all that is good. For the depressed Christian, this sense of being shut off is often interpreted as sinful alienation from God. Because they rarely recognize that depression is the cause of this painful feeling of separation, most depressed persons blame themselves. As a result, they sink even deeper into the darkness of guilt and despair. Depression is *not* a sin nor is it a reasonable cause for guilt.

Feelings of guilt often serve a healthy function in our lives. Like a "caution" or "stop" sign, they warn us about the appropriateness of the decisions we make and the actions which follow from our decisions. Guilt feelings are based on how our self concept, expectations of others, and God's inspiration are either in harmony or in conflict with the situation about which we are making a decision. Some people are paralyzed by these feelings even when making the simplest of decisions. Such an obstacle to inner freedom represents unhealthy guilt. In the depressed person's life, unhealthy guilt and failure feelings may impair healthy decisions when these feelings are based on a process tainted with distorted perceptions and thinking, with false values and unrealistic expectations.

In the depths of ourselves, in secret, we feel our unhealthy guilt. This guilt involves the frequent and uncomfortable uneasiness that we fail to live up to the expectations of our religion, of others, of society. We can be overwhelmed by our personal failures to communicate with others and with God in prayer. A common reaction when called upon to make decisions is the desire to run and hide, much like Adam did when he became aware of his nakedness and imperfection in the presence of God. In contrast, a healthy response to guilt brings the Christian to the understanding, forgiving and merciful arms of the Father. A realistic admission of our sorrow and sinfulness is very, very different from the overwhelming guilt which paralyzes so many depressed Christians. Let's take a closer look at the relationship between depression and guilt.

One of the primary effects of exaggerated guilt is an unhealthy preoccupation with one's sinfulness. Often when we are deeply depressed we feel helplessly "sin-full." As we have already discussed in an earlier chapter, depression alters our perception. Self-perception becomes so distorted that we no longer are able to see and to experience the genuine goodness of our life. In contrast, every weakness, fault and failure is magnified. This exaggeration of the negative is the inevitable result of the poor self-concept which usually accompanies depression. This deep sense of our sinful, loathsome state is portrayed by the writer of Psalm 51:

Have mercy on me, O God, in your goodness,
In your great tenderness wipe away my faults;
Wash me clean of my guilt,
Purify me from my sin.

For I am well aware of my faults,
I have my sin constantly in mind,
Having sinned against none other than you,
Having done what you regard as wrong.

You are just when you pass sentence on me,
Blameless when you give judgment.
You know I was born guilty,
A sinner from the moment of conception.

Of course we have our moments of contrition, but a life lived at this level of helplessness and guilt lacks wholeness and balance. Like Adam and Eve whose nakedness suddenly became a source of shame for them after they sinned, when we are depressed we may find ourselves painfully confronted with our dark side—that part of us which we would prefer to keep hidden from view. Our ordinary defense mechanisms which usually help to protect us from unmanageable burdens of guilt frequently fail us when we are deeply depressed. We find ourselves naked and exposed before God and in our own eyes.

The burden of guilt and poor self-esteem that accompany depression are often responsible for the mistaken conclusion that depression is itself sinful and/or the result of a sinful life. One book on depression written by a church pastor simplistically states that the cause of depression is the sin of self-pity and resentment. If only the depressed person would fall to his knees before God and ask for forgiveness of his sins, then depression would immediately and permanently depart!

A similar attitude toward depression was revealed at a recent retreat when the authors overheard a woman, during a talk on depression, whisper to her neighbor, "Good, Spirit-filled Christians don't get depressed!" Peoples' misguided attitudes place an additional burden of guilt and darkness on those among us who are depressed. We have enough problems with ourselves, not to mention these attitudes of others which make life all the more difficult!

The Darkness of Emptiness

A second common spiritual experience in depression is a profound feeling of emptiness. When we considered guilt feelings, we noted that these feelings might impair good decisions and actions. When this happens, we are left "suspended" between the guilt we feel and the decisions we feel helpless to make. It is as if we are left hanging in a wide, dark gap between the reality of our depression and what we dream or wish we could be. Such ambivalence between our depressed self and the unreachable reality to which God and others seem to call us leaves us lonely, frustrated and feeling *empty*.

In each of us there seems to be a cold, dark and unknown space. When we are not depressed we are often not aware of this fundamental and universal fact of human existence. Life seems full of potential, energy and joy, somewhat like the experience of springtime following a cold, dark winter. But when we are brought low by depression, we suddenly come face to face with an emptiness which feels as lifeless and decisionless as a frozen winter. The spiritual agony of depression is largely the result of the erroneous interpretation that this emptiness is sinful and wrong. The depressed person feels barren, at a loss for words in prayer, and abandoned by God. This experience may be extremely painful and may well lead to angry withdrawal from prayer, worship and fellowship with friends.

This void within us can only be filled and warmed by union with God. During the wintertimes of our lives when God seems so distant and we so empty, there is beneath depression the ember of God-life. Thus, each one of us must learn to deal with our own emptiness. A realistic and healthy acceptance of this deeper and seasonal aspect of our human nature can powerfully lead us to the healthy opposite of emptiness which is solitude. Beneath the winter pain of emptiness is life in the Spirit by which we naturally yearn for a closer relationship with God. Rather than struggling and striving to leap away from our present situation of emptiness, God should be invited or coaxed to join us where we are, to bring his light and warmth, and to share our winter solitude. This is perhaps the awareness of St. Augustine when he realized in his emptiness, "My heart will not rest until it rests in Thee." As Augustine accepted this reality in his life, his restless emptiness became a deeply joyful solitude in which he met and communed with God.

The Darkness of Doubt

From our emptiness, from its negative feelings of being left alone to struggle in the dark with what poor resources we have, comes the feeling of doubt. With such feelings of inner emptiness, we are not at all reassured that we will have the strength, ability and willingness to find our own way in life. We experience what it means to be left orphans. We question God's ability and his desire to bring comfort of any kind. Such is the darkness of doubt.

The following journal entry, describing this darkness, was written by a young man struggling with depression.

> Something keeps coming to mind. I keep getting a glimpse of the terror of being without God, an experience which with my senses and emotions creates a terrifying scenario. And at the same time there is a flashback to a time in my childhood—several occasions, actually—when Mother was displeased with us children and so she left us all alone. I can remember how she'd cry and say we didn't love her and so she was going to go away from us and we'd never see her again. My sister and I would plead with her not to go; we'd scream, with the tears streaming down our cheeks, that we were sorry for whatever we had done or said. We would beg her not to go. And yet I can vividly recall her walking out of the house and getting into the car—and we would run out to the driveway and pound with our fists on the car window, screaming for her not to leave us. And still she would drive away, leaving us terror-stricken that we would never see our mother again.

I'm afraid God will do this to me to punish me for my
ingratitude, for not appreciating him enough, just like Mother
punished us for not loving her enough. The thought of being
abandoned by God brings back all of the hell of being left all
alone by Mother, to scream unheard, to stand in the street
watching her drive resolutely away without even a backward
glance. . . .

When we are depressed we can no longer depend upon good,
buoyant feelings to confirm our faith. In fact, we are often totally
unable to feel God's loving presence. He seems to have vanished,
and along with him have gone all those comfortable, reassuring
indications of his blessing and his love. Where is the joy and the
peace which the Christian learns to associate with personal faith
and God's friendship? Under ordinary circumstances the Apostle
Thomas (Jn 20:19-29) was probably a faithful and happy follower
of Jesus. But during those difficult days after the resurrection he,
like the others, felt abandoned and fearful. Sentiments of joy and
peace in the Lord's presence turned to sentiments of doubt and
skepticism when Jesus was absent. Depression dims all felt awareness of the positive signs of God's life in us, and in their place rush
in doubt and confusion. The inevitable questions follow: Does God
love me? Why has God abandoned me? What terrible thing have I
done? Am I losing my faith? Can I love myself?

When we are depressed—especially if the depression is very
deep or prolonged—it may appear that every spark of faith has been
extinguished. But this is rarely the case. The mystery is that even in
the darkest, most overwhelming moments faith is alive and active
despite the numbness of our feelings. When emotional and spiritual
pain dominate our attention, we seem to lose our way which had
once seemed so certain. At such times joy and contentment with
this life are gone. Joy does not readily blossom in a climate of doubt
and skepticism. But it is precisely in the moments of disillusion-
ment and anguish of spirit that Christian faith quietly and unobtru-
sively begins to perform its work of grace. Faith is the spark, the
delicate filament of grace which anchors us to God, the Source of

light. Faith works to encourage us in the midst of depression's darkness, inspiring trust in the promises of what is unfelt and unseen.

Responses to Guilt

We all struggle in some way with the problem of sin and guilt. In our discussion of the spiritually destructive role of guilt feelings in depression, we have certainly not intended to imply that guilt is always unhealthy. A realistic acknowledgement of one's sinfulness (sorrow) may be a healthy response which leads to reconciliation, joy and growth. There is an immense difference, however, between this kind of "good" guilt and the deadly, exaggerated, preoccupied sense of sinfulness and guilt which has been described earlier.

The Apostles Peter and Judas provide good examples of the difference between healthy and unhealthy responses to guilt. In the gospel accounts of the betrayal of Jesus we read of how Judas and Peter both disowned their Master: Judas by his collusion with the chief priests and pharisees, and Peter by his thrice-repeated denial of his friendship with Jesus (Mt 24:14-16, 69-75; 27:3-10). The actions of both men created guilt—a justifiable and deep sorrow for what they had done. How each of these men chose to respond to his guilt was the decisive factor, however. Judas was overcome with regret and guilt, believing his deed to be unforgivable. In the lonely isolation of his unbearable depression Judas committed the ultimate withdrawal: suicide. On the other hand, the scriptures tell us that after his denials, Peter "went out and wept bitterly." It is not difficult to imagine the despair and agony the impetuous Peter must have felt as he wept tears of grief and repentance. But Peter's guilt did not drive him to withdrawal and destruction. He rejoined the other apostles and was among the first to run to the empty tomb on Easter morning in search of the risen Jesus. The dark cloud of Peter's threefold denial faded in the bright light of his threefold promise of service when Jesus gave him the responsibility of pastoring the church (Jn 21:15-17).

No matter how grave is one's sin, it is never too big or too terrible for the healing forgiveness of our Lord who loves us. A healthy sorrow which brings us to him in repentance is his work in us, but guilt filled with self-hate is most certainly not the work of God. We are our own most severe judges when we refuse to forgive ourselves and to accept his unconditional forgiveness which is freely offered. Recall the story of the woman taken in adultery (Jn 8:3-11). Jesus did not keep her at a distance from him with corrections and a long list of attitude and behavior changes upon which his acceptance depended. (How often we do this to ourselves and others!) Instead, Jesus looked upon her and loved and accepted her unconditionally—as she was—right at that moment. Could it be that it was his free, unconditional forgiveness and love which empowered her to go and sin no more? He treated her not as a problem but as a forgiven and loved person; that helped her to treat herself as a forgiven and loved woman. His loving kindness set her free and transformed a scene of sin, guilt and death into one of healing, freedom and love. The response of Jesus is so contrary to our own self-hate and disgust! The key to the spiritual healing of depression is the willingness to love and forgive ourselves by the light of grace, to see ourselves as he sees us, beautiful and precious and cherished.

The Light of Truth: The Need for Honesty

When we respond to the darkness in ourselves or others by adamantly insisting that "This is not Christian," or "Christians aren't this way," we are blocking avenues of grace and healing. The irony of this all-too-human response is that our "righteous" denial insures that we remain prisoners in darkness, whereas when we admit our guilt, emptiness and doubt, we take a first step in our pilgrimage toward the healing of our depression. How easy it is to be afraid when we face our darkness! One of the human reactions we experience when trying to cope with something difficult to accept is called *denial*. Denial in itself is neither good nor bad. What is important is whether we recognize it or not, and how we then respond to it. This reaction can be so strong that our memory may simply "go blank," or we may be at a loss for words, or we may not comprehend what is so clear to others. When we experience this kind of unintentional "resistance" to facing something, we can be assured that a sensitive area of our life in need of healing and freedom is being touched.

Healing and freedom are inseparably united to honesty. There can be no genuine freedom where truth is denied. As we seek to be healed, we make a firm commitment to the truth, for when in the bondage of our depression we open the door to the light of truth, the most decisive step of our journey has been taken. Let's consider for a minute just what it means to "walk in the truth."

On the most basic level, walking in the truth means being honest with ourselves—acknowledging and dealing with those difficult, usually negative areas in our lives. It means facing the fact that at times we are depressed, we are unreasonable, we are confused, we are stubborn. This points to our absolute need to grow in self-trust and become less discouraged about ourselves. All of us have a dark side which we prefer to keep hidden from the view of others—and also from ourselves. Perhaps because of our false ideas of what it means to be a Christian we do not want that part of us confronted which is in darkness and which needs healing. Our denial reactions continue to keep our guilt, emptiness and doubt hidden from our very own awareness! But before we can move on to other areas of truth, we must resolve to be as honest and as kind as possible with ourselves.

Secondly, we must be honest with God. How much we are like Adam and Eve: part of us knows full well that we cannot hide ourselves from God yet we still try to shield from him those parts of us which are not pretty, which are dark. But how can our Physician heal us if we hide our disease from him? When we are honest with ourselves about our unhealed and unattractive selves, we will be able to be honest with our God. Many depressed people who have developed customary habits of prayer throughout their lives find this kind of honesty difficult. With the darkness of depression comes an inability to find words or verbal ways to share oneself deeply with God. When words fail, one might attempt to pray using non-verbal images, pictures of the mind and heart. When imagination also fails to communicate in prayer, one may just *be* there in God's presence just as one is and as one feels or fails to feel. Such is indeed being honest with God.

Thirdly, we must strive for honesty in our relationships with others. Some of this honesty involves sympathetically informing people when the advice they give seems inaccurate, unrealistic or wrong. Similarly, we need to make efforts to hear and to experience the truth from others who are growing in the art of pure caring. Walking in the truth means we must gradually gain the courage to put aside our masks. As we grow in our desire for freedom, we will grow in our ability to hear the truth about ourselves from *trusted* friends. As we experience more inner freedom we have the courage to be who and what we are—healed yet needing healing.

Sometimes in our churches and Christian communities it becomes a fearful thing to speak of or to receive those parts of us that are as yet unhealed. And so we unintentionally block the saving, healing work of God because we do not welcome or bring the very parts of ourselves most in need. As we guard our secret darkness, we not only make room for guilt feelings in ourselves but we unwittingly nurture them in others. Darkness borne alone will crush us, but when in a climate of compassion and trust we share our dark sides with others we all grow and our burdens become lighter. What a blessing it would be if we could share our lives so completely that we would be as free to reveal our darkness to others as we are to reveal our light. Only when we can begin to do this will we be able to assist one another in our journey from depression to healing.

Prayer in Darkness

> "Turn your eyes upon Jesus,
> Look full in his wonderful face,
> And the things of earth will grow strangely dim
> In the light of his glory and grace."

So goes a simple chorus learned long ago in Sunday School. There is a powerful, powerful truth in these short lines: when we keep our eyes fixed upon Jesus, our burdens come into perspective and are no longer the unbearable loads we thought they were. There may be many, many nights when we are unable to utter any other prayer than just a short refrain such as this; depression often deadens us so that we feel incapable of articulate, heartfelt prayer. At such times it may be helpful to recall that to be where we are right now in his presence is to be safe from every terror of darkness; even the horrors of our own dark selves cannot overcome us in his presence because he is stronger than even these. Keep your eyes on Jesus: how sad it is that we often reject such simple truths because they seem too simple, too pat, too unrealistic. Keep the eyes of your heart, mind and spirit on Jesus.

Peter discovered in a dramatic way the power of keeping his eyes on Jesus (Mt 14:25-33). When devoted but impetuous Peter saw Jesus walking on the water toward the apostles' boat one stormy night on the Sea of Galilee, he jumped out of the boat and started walking across the water to Jesus. But the gospels tell us that when Peter felt the force of the wind and the waves he became afraid and began to sink. Before he took his eyes off Jesus he was doing just fine, but the minute he shifted his attention from Jesus to the storm around him and to his own fears, he was in trouble. We are like this, too. Depression can have all of the disorienting, frightening force of a storm at sea: the negative thinking, the distorted view of self, God and the world, and the undependable emotions which have us in tears one moment and deathly numb the next.

All of these disorienting aspects of depression demand our

attention. Our personal safety seems at stake. Before going any further, it is important to stress that this tendency toward self-consciousness is not the same thing as self-centeredness, neither is it the deliberate turning away from Jesus that we call sin. It is not these at all. Rather, it is a very natural, human response to pain. In depression we concentrate on what hurts and how we seem lost and this makes it much more difficult to concentrate on other things. We can become easily confused and distracted. But in the midst of such inner insecurity, we *are* in the presence of Jesus. Our darkness is prayer. Our anger, resentment, and fury are true emotions and they communicate our real feelings to God. This honest communication is the ''stuff'' of an intimate, deep relationship with God.

It would be naive to think that it is easy to keep one's eyes focused on Jesus. There are times when it feels nearly impossible. The dark thoughts of depression have a way of overpowering our perception and good judgment. Particularly when we are depressed and feel distant from God's love and blessing, it is difficult to pray. Is he still there? Will he hear my prayer? Does he love me? Questions like these crowd into our mind, and when feelings of emptiness, sinfulness and abandonment fill us, we may feel that prayer is futile or even unwelcome. But when we are in darkness, the single most important thing we can do is pray. And that means being ourselves with God.

There is a little story which may help to give some insight into the problem of prayer in darkness. The story is about a small child who is caught on the second floor of a burning house. All alone and terrified, he stands at the bedroom window and cries out for help. On the ground below him stands his father. ''Jump, son, and I'll catch you,'' the father calls out. ''But I can't see you, daddy, I can't see you! I'll fall, daddy!'' The child, frightened, refuses to budge from his precarious position because smoke has so irritated his eyes and obscured his vision that he cannot see his father who is waiting below with outstretched hands. ''But son, *I* can see *you*,'' the father calls out. ''Jump and I will catch you.''

How often we are like this frightened child! Because we do not *feel* that God is there, we conclude that he is not, and so we remain in our depression and fear because we are unwilling to make the leap of faith into his arms. Jesus is always there. No matter how depressed, how sinful, how doubtful, how empty we are—Jesus is *always* there, waiting for us with outstretched arms. When we are depressed we must learn to stop relying on our feelings and instead rely on our faith. Our feelings are *not* reliable indicators when we are depressed.

On the night before he died Jesus spoke these reassuring words:

> Do not let your hearts be troubled.
> Have faith in God and faith in me.
> In my Father's house there are many dwelling places;
> Otherwise, how could I have told you
> That I was going to prepare a place for you?
> I am indeed going to prepare a place for you,
> And then I shall come back to take you with me,
> That where I am you also may be.
> You know the way that leads where I go.

> "Lord," said Thomas, we do not know where you are going. How can we know the way?"

> Jesus told him:
> "I am the way, and the truth, and the life!" (Jn 14:1-6a).

Faith is inseparably united to trust; to have faith is to trust the word of another, in spite of how we feel or the fact that we cannot see for ourselves where we are going. Scripture assures us that no matter what, we will never be abandoned by God.

Prayer in depression is prayer in darkness. The prayer of the depressed person calls out into the darkness, "My God, my God, why have you forsaken me?" It is prayer in darkness which echoes the humble entreaty of the publican in the outer court of the Temple: "Lord, have mercy on me, a sinner!" It is a lonely cry in the night. It is the whispered plea for reassurance that one has not really been abandoned, that one is still loved by God, and that he is near. Prayer in darkness, though, is a prayer that no loving Father can resist. Turn your eyes upon Jesus.

Depression and the Cross

There seems to be absolutely no way to talk about the problem of depression without also talking about the presence of the cross in the life of Jesus Christ. The cross brings us to the suffering Jesus. His suffering and death may not be ignored or denied from his life. In the garden he prayed, "Father, if you are willing, take this cup away from me. Nevertheless, let your will be done, not mine" (Lk 22:42).

It was on the cross he said, "I am thirsty," (Jn 19:28) and "Father, forgive them, they do not know what they are doing" (Lk 23:34).

He then said, "My God, my God, why have you deserted me?" (Mk 15:34) and, as he breathed his last, "Father, into your hands I commit my Spirit" (Lk 23:46). His obedience, courage, love and honesty during such suffering are outstanding examples.

There is no hint of enjoyment or pretense in what he experienced. He suffered to the point of death. He felt the abandonment and darkness mentioned in this chapter. These feelings are acceptable. He clearly showed us that by his own witness.

Most of us would probably rather not think too long about the cross in our own lives; after all, the cross brings with it all of the very unpleasant ideas of disappointment, betrayal, suffering and death. All of us would rather be exclusively "Easter People"— we'd rather focus on the sunshine and joy of the resurrection than we would on the darkness of Calvary. But consider the cross we must. Not only is it planted firmly in the center of the mystery of faith, but it is a personal reality for every one of us and ignoring it will not make it go away.

Crosses come in all sizes, shapes and varieties. The crosses we bear may be what we think of as "big" ones: the loss of a loved one, chronic loneliness, a crippling disease, poverty, an unhappy marriage, a retarded child, deep depression. Or our crosses may be "little" ones: the disappointments we experience, the shortcomings we are aware of, the opportunities that we pass up, the disagreements, misunderstandings and rivalries that inevitably occur when people get together with people. Actually, although we commonly compare our crosses with those of others, there is no real way that we can measure suffering or say that one person's suffering is more or less than another's.

Austrian psychiatrist Viktor Frankl compares suffering to the behavior of gas. If a certain amount of gas is pumped into an empty chamber, it will fill the chamber completely and evenly, no matter how big the chamber. In the same way, he observes, suffering completely fills the human spirit and conscious mind, no matter whether the suffering is "great" or "little."[1] Depression is a form of suffering and it, too, is like the gas of which Frankl speaks. It completely affects us as persons regardless of its intensity. But big or little, the depression in our lives brings us face to face with the reality of our need for healing, our need for others, our need for God. We are confronted with the cross, and we can choose whether we will fight it or accept it. Either way, the cross will always be present in our lives.

Reflecting on his experiences in the Nazi concentration camps, Viktor Frankl concludes that one of the most powerful tactics for dealing with suffering is to transform it into sacrifice.[2] Suffering tends to trap us in self; sacrifice frees us from ourselves. This is a critical point for all who experience the darkness of suffering and pain. The important reality is this: either we may become so ensnared, alienated and bitter in our suffering that life is misery for ourselves and others, or we may actively and wholeheartedly bring ourselves, with our anguish and hurt, to the foot of the cross. There in the presence of Jesus we experience and identify with a Saving Lord who converts suffering into sacrifice. Joyful people have a way of bringing delight to others. Peaceful people bring a deep sense of comfort. Resentful people raise thoughts of dissatisfaction. Bitter people alienate others. Our response to suffering, whether it be negative or positive, is contagious and profoundly affects the lives of others around us. The supreme example of suffering becoming sacrifice is that the hour of Jesus' greatest suffering was the occasion of his sacrifice for us. He remained conscious of his Father's will and spoke words of forgiveness for us all. His redemptive response to suffering signalled our salvation and provides a model for us.

Sacrifice has meaning because it unites us with others; through sacrifice others are somehow helped. It is extremely difficult to hold up under great suffering when it seems to have no purpose or meaning. But once the individual can see a meaning for his suffering, it becomes easier to endure. As the philosopher Nietzsche said, if we know the *why*, we can live with almost any *how*. While sacrifice provides meaning for suffering, it will always remain a mystery.

Sacrifice also implies freedom. Our suffering is not sacrifice unless it is something that we freely offer. As long as we rebel, we are not offering sacrifice. But when we actively surrender our pain into the hands of God, trusting his word that "all things work together for good to those that love God" (Rm 8:28), we find meaning through faith. Thus, sacrifice means more than enduring suffering. It is an active gift of oneself by which one *overcomes*. No matter how dark life is for us, we are always free to choose how we will respond to that darkness. Though we may not be able to choose the circumstances of our life, as we become healed we are more able to choose our attitude toward those circumstances. Whatever the personal meaning may be that each one of us finds within our own suffering, it can lend us the courage that we so desperately need to carry our cross and to experience victory.

Each one of us has our own passover experiences. There are nights when it seems that daylight will never come again; there are times when we are sure that we will never again know the joy of his presence or a day without depression. Jesus has called us to share in his life: and in so doing he has called us to the garden of Gethsemane, to Pilate's judgment hall, and to Calvary. Jesus said, "If you would be my disciple, you must pick up your cross and follow me." At the cross he invites us to join him and his mother who stayed with him, her heart broken with pain. When we struggle with the cross in our lives—whether it be depression or any other suffering—we identify with Jesus in a very personal, special way. We can be assured of his continual presence to us. More than that, we can be comforted by the others who were with him during his suffering and death. He called upon God the Father. He had the presence of his mother's love. She could not take his place but her presence was important to him. John stood with Mary at the foot of the cross. How important that presence is for us—the presence of God, loved ones and friends! Even when suffering actually extinguishes the awareness of that presence, the knowing it was always there helps pull us out of the depression when the worst pain begins to subside.

Words of Light in Darkness

The Psalms are a treasury filled with words of encouragement for the suffering, the troubled, and the lost. No strangers to the darkness of depression, the writers of the Psalms vividly express the struggle within the heart of the person of faith. The word of God in scripture has a unique, unparalleled power to nourish and sustain us. As we have tried to portray in this chapter, the depressed person is so overcome with the darkness of guilt, emptiness and doubt that it is difficult to concentrate on prayer. When we are distracted by pain and confusion, we need something very simple to hang onto. Just the simple repetition throughout the day of a one-sentence prayer is often enough to help us keep in touch with God. The following are some simple, one-line prayers from the Psalms that may be helpful.

You never desert those who seek you, Yahweh (Ps 9:10).

*   *   *

Look after me, God, I take shelter in you (Ps 16:1).

* * *

I keep Yahweh before me always, for with him at my right hand nothing can shake me (Ps 16:8).

* * *

Yahweh, you yourself are my lamp, my God lights up my darkness (Ps 18:28).

* * *

Yahweh is my light and my salvation, whom need I fear? (Ps 27:1).

* * *

Yahweh is my strength, my shield, my heart puts its trust in him (Ps 28:7).

* * *

You are a hiding place for me, you guard me when in trouble (Ps 46:1).

* * *

God is our shelter, our strength, ever ready to help in time of trouble (Ps 46:1).

* * *

Have mercy on me, O God, in your goodness; in your great tenderness wipe away my faults (Ps 51:1).

* * *

God, create a clean heart in me, put into me a new and constant spirit (Ps 51:10).

* * *

Unload your burdens onto Yahweh and he will support you (Ps 55:22).

* * *

In God alone there is rest for my soul, from him comes my safety (Ps 62:1).

* * *

My refuge, my fortress, my God in whom I trust (Ps 91:2).

*   *   *

Your word is a lamp to my feet, a light on my path (Ps 119:105).

Footnotes

1. Viktor E. Frankl, *Man's Search for Meaning* (New York: Pocket Books, 1963), p. 69-70.
2. Frankl, p. 179.

CHAPTER SEVEN

MEDICAL ASPECTS OF DEPRESSION

Depression is a disorder which affects one emotionally and psychologically, spiritually, and physically. We have already carefully examined the psychological and spiritual ramifications of depression, and will now turn to its physical aspects. An understanding of the physiological or body mechanisms which underlie our mood states provides insight into both the biological causes and treatment for depression. Current theories of the physical bases of depression will be considered, followed by a discussion of medical treatment approaches, particularly the modern antidepressant drugs, and electroshock therapy. We will begin with the stories of two young depressed women.

Two Illustrative Case Histories

Elizabeth is an elementary schoolteacher and a divorced mother with one daughter, who was living in a Christian community when she came to me (Dick) for help. Elizabeth had been feeling tired and uninterested in life and very much wanted to feel otherwise. She did not know how to change her dim and helpless outlook. Without being able to pinpoint the exact cause of her dejection, she knew that something was wrong with her way of thinking and that this mental and physical fatigue was affecting every aspect of her life, her work, and her relationships with others. All of this raised fears in her that she was losing her mind. Elizabeth had made great exhausting efforts to keep up with her work and her family and community life, but she found herself drained of energy and ready to give up. The result of this snowballing chain of events was that she felt extremely guilty and fearful because she couldn't measure up to what she felt she "should" be, the ideals by which she was trying to live. This was the tale of frustration which she poured out in our conversation together.

After talking with her for awhile I recognized that Elizabeth was describing depression. We spoke then about the nature of depression, and in the course of our discussion I suggested that biological imbalances can and do have profound effects on how we think and feel, and that these imbalances can be corrected with medication. It was hard to convince Elizabeth that something which so affects one's thoughts can be biologically based, but when she began to understand this, she seemed instantly relieved and brightened with new hope. Later, she told me it was a great relief to know she wasn't losing her mind after all, and that something positive could be done to relieve many of the symptoms of depression, especially the mental and physical fatigue commonly experienced by depressed people.

I recommended that Elizabeth consult her physician, which she did. Her doctor prescribed antidepressant medication, and the regimen of medication plus daily exercise (jogging) produced marked improvement of her depression. She found new strength for and interest in her teaching and her family and community life.

Sally is a young wife and mother of three small children. Sally had not been feeling well for quite some time, suffering from continual fatigue, headaches, and other vague discomforts. Like many depressed people, she could not identify exactly what her problem was. When she went to see her physician, he prescribed antidepressant medication.

Sally called me (Chris) later that day, and was upset and

confused about her visit with the doctor and by his diagnosis of depression. She was surprised when her doctor concluded that the cause of her tiredness and aches was depression. It was even more upsetting for her to be told she would need medication for the depression. The notion that there was something amiss in her body chemistry which could produce depression was frightening for her, and somehow made depression seem more serious. What seemed to bother her the most was the inference that she was "mentally ill." She knew that patients in mental hospitals were given medication, and it was unsettling to think that what her doctor felt she needed was this same kind of medication.

I talked with Sally for a long while, answering her many questions about depression, its causes—including biological causes—and the use of drugs to treat depression. Our conversation relieved many of her fears, and Sally wisely decided she would take the medication that her doctor had prescribed for her. Within a few weeks Sally reported that she was feeling much better.

The stories of Elizabeth and Sally illustrate how the same information-that physical, biochemical imbalances affect how we think and feel-can produce very different feelings and responses in people. The reason for this difference seems to be related to the care (or lack of care) taken to provide a clear but complete explanation. Once an understanding of the biological basis of depression is achieved, many fears and misconceptions are dispelled. Because we have seen how vital this understanding can be, the remainder of this chapter has been devoted to a discussion of the biological and medical aspects of depression.

Physical Aspects of Depression

The human body is a marvelously intricate machine. Each of its many systems is designed to work in harmony with all other systems. When the body's organs and systems are functioning well, health is the result. Sometimes, however, the body is unable to function well because of an inherited defect, an injury, or an imbalance within or among its many parts. When this happens, the individual experiences poor health—he does not feel well.

Our emotional and psychological health is influenced by the functioning of our physical body. When something is amiss physically, our perception, thinking, feelings and behavior are usually affected in some way. There are a number of physical disturbances which are known to be related to depression. Although much research must yet be done before we will be able to clearly understand and correct these physical irregularities, there is sufficient evidence to conclude that genetic factors, hormone levels, mineral metabolism, stress, and biochemical imbalances are all involved in depression.

Genetic factors. Many studies have been conducted in an effort to determine whether or not depression has a hereditary basis. At the present time there appears to be sufficient evidence to strongly suggest that certain kinds of depression, manic-depressive or "bipolar" disease, can be inherited. A consistent finding in the studies performed throughout the world has been that the likelihood of developing this type of depression is about twenty times greater among close relatives (parents, children, brothers and sisters) of someone with a bipolar disorder than that of the general population. This sounds ominous, but it must be remembered that most forms of depression are *not* thought to be inherited; and even for those that are, only a tendency or *predisposition* is inherited. Other factors, such as environment, learned coping skills, and personal relationships, may play a strong part in determining whether or not an individual will be vulnerable to the tendency to develop the disease even if the genes were inherited. Those specific forms of depression which are believed to have a genetic basis are related to biochemical imbalances and, with medication, can be readily controlled.

Hormonal factors. A powerful system of the body known as the *endocrine* system includes the various glands that secrete hormones into the bloodstream. Imbalances in the levels of hormones produced by several of the endocrine glands often result in alterations in mood and may lead to mild or even severe depression. Of particular importance in this regard are imbalances of the steroid hormones manufactured by the adrenal glands, thyroid hormones, and some of the secretions of the pituitary gland. There is also considerable evidence that changes in sex hormone function may also affect mood, although the problem is probably more complex than a simple increase or decrease in the level of particular hormone. Women are especially vulnerable to depression at times of endocrine change: premenstrually, post-partum, at the menopause, or in association with oral contraceptives.

A part of the brain known as the *hypothalamus* regulates, through a complex feedback system, the levels of many of the hormones of the endocrine glands. The hypothalamus also regulates appetite, sexual activity, the menstrual cycle, and aggression, all of which may be disturbed in persons suffering from depression. Disorders of the hypothalamus may produce intense emotional highs and lows, and thus the functioning of this part of the brain and its interaction with the endocrine system is important in the understanding of depression.

Mineral metabolism. Basic to the functioning of the body is the balance of minerals such as sodium, potassium, magnesium, and calcium. These minerals, which are called *electrolytes*, play a key role in the transmission of nerve messages from one nerve cell to the next. Research indicates that the functioning of these electrolytes, especially sodium, is disturbed in persons who suffer from depression. (This is especially true in manic-depressive disease. Lithium, a drug which is frequently prescribed for manic-depressives, is believed to correct the imbalances of minerals in the nervous system.)

Stress. When the body is subjected to stress—such as pregnancy, an infection, surgery, a traumatic experience, trouble on the job, an incompatible marriage, etc.—a series of response mechanisms are triggered to help cope with the stress. Hormones are poured into the bloodstream and the nervous system is "activated." Sometimes this response is excessive or prolonged, and nervous exhaustion and depression may follow.

Medication. Almost all drugs have "side effects"—undesirable physical or psychological actions which are not central to their primary purpose. A common example of this is the upset stomach that is sometimes caused by ordinary aspirin. Some drugs are known to produce depression as a side efect in persons who are predisposed to depression. When this happens, the doctor usually discontinues the medication which is causing the problem and substitutes another one which may not have such severe side effects.

The Biochemical Roots of Depression

Although it is far more complex, the human brain is often compared to a sophisticated modern computer. Like a computer, the brain possesses millions of tiny circuits through which electrically coded messages are transmitted. All life processes—from the simplest to the most complex—depend upon the brain's ability to communicate with the rest of the body both by sending and receiving messages which allow the human person to maintain fundamental biological functions, to act, feel and think. The smallest elements or cells of the intricate communication network of the nervous system are called *neurons*. Each neuron, which is so tiny that it usually can be seen only with the aid of a microscope, makes contact with another neuron at a junction which is called the *synapse*. The synapse is a microscopic gap between neurons, across which the nerve message is sent via special chemicals known as *neurotransmitters*. Researchers in the fields of neuropsychology and neuropsychiatry believe that the action of neurotransmitters at the synapses in the brain and spinal cord hold the key to a variety of emotional and psychological disorders—including depression.

Several neurotransmitters have been identified in the brain, and at least two of these are believed to play an important role in depression. These chemicals, which are manufactured, stored, released, used, and then rendered chemically inactive in the brain, are called *norepinephrine* (also known as *noradrenaline*) and *serotonin*. While the exact ways by which norepinephrine and serotonin are related to depression are still unknown, ongoing medical research has demonstrated beyond any doubt that the level and balance of these two chemicals can markedly affect emotional states such as depression and mania (excessive elation and excitement). Heredity, hormone levels, and electrolyte balance, which have been discussed earlier, may all interact to affect the balance and function of these neurotransmitters.

A detailed discussion of the biochemistry of depression is beyond the scope of this book. Briefly, however, research indicates that decreased levels of available norepinephrine, serotonin, or both, tend to produce depression. Medical authorities believe these biochemical changes can be a cause of depression. Also, the lack of physical activity, so characteristic of depressed persons, may tend to reduce production of norepinephrine in the brain and spinal cord. The major medical treatments for depression, antidepressant medications and electroshock therapy, are effective because for as yet unexplained reasons they increase the amount of norepinephrine and serotonin at the synapse in the brain. As these neurotransmitters are brought back into proper balance the distressing symptoms of depression are gradually lifted.

Medical Treatment of Depression

MEDICATIONS

Modern research in the use of drugs for the treatment of depression began in the 1950's as the result of serendipity. It all began when some astute physicians noticed that patients being given a drug for tuberculosis experienced an improvement in mood along with increased energy and a sense of well-being. Other TB patients in the same wards who were not receiving this particular medication did not manifest any emotional changes. Their scientific curiosity aroused, medical researchers began a long series of investigations which eventually culminated in the development of the first antidepressant drugs, which are known as the "MAO Inhibitors." Since that time a number of drugs in the MAO Inhibitor family have come into use. Some of the more common ones include (by brand name) Nardil, Marplan, Niamid, Parnate, and Eutonyl. As a group these drugs are often called "psychic energizers," and are thought to exert their antidepressant effect by altering and balancing the levels of neurotransmitters in the brain. Thus, MAO Inhibitors can be very effective in treating some kinds of depression. Like all antidepressant medications, these drugs can only be obtained by a physician's prescription, and it is essential that the doctor's instructions are followed regarding necessary dietary restrictions and the avoidance of other medicines that have not been prescribed while taking MAO Inhibitor antidepressant drugs.

Although the MAO Inhibitors are sometimes prescribed, drugs of a second major type, the "tricyclics," are used more often. The most common tricyclic antidepressants include (by brand name): Tofranil, Elavil, Norpramin, Pertofrane, Aventyl, Pamelor, Vivactil, and Sinequan. These too are believed to correct the biochemical imbalances which seemingly produce depression.

Most of the medications prescribed for depression, both MAO Inhibitors and the tricyclics, require about 10 to 14 days to take effect. Because of this, it is very important not to "give up" too early and stop taking the medication before it has had time to become effective. If after three or four weeks there has been no improvement, the doctor may want to change to another antidepressant drug. People respond differently to these drugs, and changing medication or dosage to find the one that works best is common practice.

Another thing that is helpful to know about antidepressants is that certain side effects may occur. Every medicine can produce unwanted side effects, and the antidepressants are no exception. The most commonly encountered side effects are dry mouth, drowsiness, lowered blood pressure, water retention, skin rash, sweating, constipation, and changes in heart rhythm. Usually these side effects are mild and disappear after a few days or weeks. Severe and persistent effects, of course, should be reported to the doctor. In general, the tricyclic antidepressants are considered to be very safe drugs.

Perhaps one of the most important mottos for the depressed person regarding medication is "Do not give up." It is worth putting up with the dry mouth and drowsiness that sometimes occur in the first ten days of treatment. The drug needs time to work—at least two or three weeks—so it is important to follow the doctor's directions. Last but not least, be sure to heed the doctor's advice about when it is time to stop taking the antidepressant medication, as Sally's experience clearly illustrates.

During the initial period of drug treatment, Sally needed encouragement from others to stay on her prescribed medication. The drowsiness which she experienced in the first week was terribly annoying for a busy mother with three young children. This side effect soon disappeared, and as the medicine began to take effect, Sally's depression, fatigue and headaches also began to disappear. In a few weeks she reported that she felt much better physically, had more energy, and enjoyed a more optimistic view of life. She was also pleased that her spiritual life had become more satisfying than it had been in months, when it was hampered by her depression.

Six weeks or so after Sally began taking her medication she was feeling so well she thought she could get along fine without it. Without consulting her physician, Sally discontinued her antidepressant; two weeks later she found herself struggling to fight off crying spells. For no apparent reason, she was back in the pit of depression. Her body's response at this early stage of treatment was a very clear illustration of the biochemical roots of many kinds of depression. I (Chris) advised her to resume her medication at once, and she was soon feeling like herself again. It is not unusual for people to take an antidepressant for three months or even a year or longer in order to prevent the depression from reoccurring, and, hopefully, to allow the body to regain its own ability to regulate the level and balance of its neurotransmitters.

Despite the fact that antidepressant medication is effective in relieving some kinds of depression, people suffering from this disorder sometimes resist the idea of medication for a variety of reasons. One common reason is the fear, as Sally expressed it, that the need for medication is a confirmation that one is "mentally ill." There is a natural resistance to taking the same kind of medication that "psychiatric patients" take. In our society a stigma is still associated with psychiatric treatment, and this makes some people reluctant to seek and follow through with treatment for "emotional difficulties"—including depression.

While this kind of reasoning above is based on the notion that depression is only a psychiatric problem, another idea—that depression is a purely spiritual problem—can produce an equally strong resistance to medication. Some well-meaning but misguided Christians reject the use of medication (and psychotherapy, too for that matter), insisting that the depressed Christian should go to the Lord for strength and healing. They imply that these other sources of assistance are unnecessary and inappropriate for the believer. This "religious reasoning" is often accompanied by the belief that drugs which affect one's mood and mind would not be approved by God. In effect, however, all antidepressant drugs are prescribed to correct *physical, biochemical imbalances* which in turn have a profound impact on feelings.

The fear of drug abuse and becoming dependent on drugs is another reason why some people are resistant to the idea of taking medication to relieve depression. In the past, amphetamines ("speed") were prescribed for people who suffered from depression, but these potentially habit-forming drugs are no longer used for this purpose today. Modern antidepressant drugs do *not* produce physical dependence (addiction) and are rarely if ever abused. One reason for this is because, unlike the drugs which are commonly abused (legally and illegally), tricyclics and MAO Inhibitors have *no* mood effects on "normal" persons who do not have the biochemical imbalances of depression. It is not possible to get "high" on antidepressants.

Another common source of resistance to medication is the initial occurrence of side effects which we have already mentioned. The drowsiness, dry mouth, and other annoying physical effects of the medication may tempt some people to stop taking their medicine after only a few days. Part of the problem is that people are often unprepared for these side effects because their physician may fail to mention them. Because the antidepressant relief does not usually become apparent for seven to ten days, it is understandable why one would decide to abandon a treatment which does not seem to be working and which has annoying side effects as well. Again, the important thing here is "Do not give up."

Lastly, the cost of medication may be a deterring factor for some individuals. Prescription drugs are usually not cheap, and antidepressants, unfortunately, are no exception. However, most health insurance plans do include such medicines among covered medical expenses.

If one is told that medication is necessary to correct a heart disorder, there is usually no question as to whether such medicine is fitting of the Christian, or if it is worth the expense or annoying side effects. Medication for depression, which like heart disease is a condition with a definite physical basis, should not be different.

ELECTROSHOCK THERAPY

In addition to antidepressant medication another form of physical therapy used in the treatment of depression is electroshock therapy (sometimes referred to as "EST," "ECT," or "ECS"). Electroshock has been known since the 1930's to be effective in producing rapid relief of depression, and while for a number of years it declined in use it is now being prescribed more often. Many doctors prefer to reserve electroshock therapy for severe depressions and those depressions which are not responding to other treatment approaches. The speed with which shock treatment works has led to its use specifically when there is thought to be severe danger of suicide. Like the various drugs which are effective in relieving depression, electroshock is believed to exert its therapeutic action by restoring the balance of essential chemicals in the brain, although the precise mechanism by which electroshock works is unknown. Because electroshock is little understood by medical science and because of the possibility that it may produce lasting effects on the brain, it remains a highly controversial method of therapy. This does not automatically mean, however, that it should not be considered if recommended by an experienced psychiatrist.

As it is administered in modern hospitals, electroshock therapy is not particularly unpleasant or dangerous. The most disturbing and in some cases apparently permanent side effect of electroshock therapy is the disruption of memory which almost always occurs after several treatments. Memories for events within the last weeks or even months prior to treatment are forgotten; in many cases most of these forgotten memories eventually come back on their own. Depression usually begins to lift after two or three treatments; the ordinary procedure is to administer a series of six to ten treatments. If the physician advises electroshock therapy in order to relieve severe depression, it should be discussed in light of the alternatives available and with consideration of the potential after-effects which may result from this medical treatment.

Psychological Treatment of Depression: Psychotherapy

Medical forms of treatment for depression, such as medication and electroshock therapy, have proven their effectiveness and value. Many persons who suffer from depression have been helped by the medical approach. It would be a grave mistake, however, to conclude that medical science possesses a quick and easy panacea. There are no sure-fire cure-alls, no magic pills, no guaranteed words of medical wisdom which will forever banish depression from one's life. It is because of this that we have consistently advocated throughout this book a holistic approach to the healing of depression. In line with this approach, it is appropriate to consider the role of psychotherapy in the management of depression.

The term "psychotherapy" is loosely applied to a wide variety of "helping" situations. Whether the psychotherapist is a psychiatrist (M.D.), a clinical psychologist (Ph.D.), a social worker (M.S.W.), or a paraprofessional counselor, psychotherapy is based upon a relationship between two persons: One (the depressed person) who is seeking to change something about oneself, and the other (the therapist) who is recognized as having the skills needed to assist with the mental change process.

Depending upon the school of thought in which he or she has been trained, the therapist will utilize any of a number of different approaches. These may include talking over one's feelings in order to gain insight into problems, perhaps probing memories of past events which may be contributing to the present depression. Sometimes perceptions and thought patterns are carefully examined and challenged to help free one from negative thinking habits which keep one depressed. Interpersonal relationships with one's family members, friends, and co-workers are very often reviewed because relationships can be either a source of encouragement and support or a source of conflict and depression. Because of the central role played by our interactions with others, group therapy is often suggested as helpful in learning new social skills and in assisting one to see that others share many of the same fears and difficulties.

The most healing aspect of psychotherapy is the relationship of trust, support, and unconditional acceptance which it promotes. This relationship in therapy between the therapist and the depressed person stands at the heart of the therapeutic process. Therapy can provide a safe and objective forum in which one may explore without fear new, more healthy styles of coping with life and life's difficulties.

Like all other approaches to the healing of depression, psychotherapy works best when it is combined with other tactics. Medication, for example, is rarely prescribed in isolation, but is extremely effective when it is used along with a program of psychotherapy. Recent psychiatric research has revealed that psychotherapy and antidepressant medication, when used together, are clearly more effective than when either one is used alone. Especially when one is severely depressed, electroshock and/or antidepressant drugs can quickly relieve the worst of the depression so that the individual can receive the most benefit from psychotherapy. Then in psychotherapy one can begin to deal with the factors in one's relationships, one's environment, and one's past experiences that are creating or maintaining the depression.

Reliance on medication alone—without at the same time working to change the depression-causing elements in one's life— usually does not lead to lasting healing of depression. The *whole* person—body, mind, and spirit—suffers from depression, and the *whole* person is in need of healing. Thus the most effective program of healing is concerned with the medical, psychological, and spiritual aspects of depression.

Spiritual Dimensions of Therapy

Just as psychotherapy or counseling is recommended along with the medical therapies, the Christian will also recognize the need for collaborative "spiritual therapy." Pastoral counseling and prayer for inner healing can help the Christian suffering from depression to trust in God when the darkness of guilt, doubt, and confusion threaten to overwhelm. Also, the loving support and encouragement of Christian friends is of great importance for the depressed person and for relatives and friends who are attempting to help. It is particularly essential that Christians not *oppose* medical treatment or psychotherapy. Without treatment, the illness of depression can so darken one's vision of life that spiritual growth is retarded. Thus a moderately or severely depressed individual must have professional care in addition to the ministry of the Christian community.

In the Gospels we read in the accounts of Jesus' healing ministry that he often sent lepers to the priests to be diagnosed and declared "clean" (cf. Mt 8:4; Mk 1:43-44; Lk 5:14, 17:14). In this Jesus followed the Mosaic Law which in those days delegated to priests the responsibility and authority to identify sickness and to proclaim restoration of health (cf. Lv 13, entire chapter). In our times this diagnostic role is assumed by the physician and the psychologist. Health care professionals—the physician, the psychiatrist, the psychologist—are instruments of God's healing power, and clearly have a place in the healing ministry for the Christian.

MEDITATION ON THE PHYSICIAN'S ROLE

Honor the doctor with the honor that is his due
        in return for his services;
            for he too has been created by the Lord.
Healing itself comes from the Most High,
        like a gift from a king.
The doctor's learning keeps his head high,
        he is regarded with awe by potentates.
The Lord has brought medicines into existence
        from the earth, and the sensible man
        will not despise them.
Did not a piece of wood once sweeten the water,
        thus giving proof of its virtue?
He has also given men learning
        so that they may glory in his mighty works.
He uses them to heal and to relieve pain,
        the chemist makes up a mixture from them.
Thus there is no end to his activities,
        and through him health extends across the world.
Let the doctor take over—the Lord created him too—
        and do not let him leave you,
            for you need him (Ec 38:1-8, 12).

CHAPTER EIGHT

EXERCISE, NUTRITION & DEPRESSION

The struggle with depression or suffering of any kind often brings forth difficult questions from the heart of one who is seeking to understand and to cope with pain. Bewildered and desperate, the depressed person questions God: "Why are you doing this to me?" "Why me?" With time, one is able to see that God Himself does not send depression or suffering to His children. Such questions about suffering test faith severely and in the end may leave one unsatisfied until at last a new question emerges: "Lord, what do you expect *me* to do about this problem?" The focus has changed. The emergence of this question signifies a turning toward healing. No longer trapped in an attitude of utter helplessness, the sufferer now is ready to consider what *he* can do to help himself. He musters strength and courage. "Be of good courage and he will strengthen your heart" (Ps 31:24).

Depression is a condition which fosters passivity. The depressed person is physically, mentally, and spiritually slowed down. This, together with the fatigue and withdrawal which so often accompany depression, strengthens the tendency to inactivity. When finally the depressed person is able to consider what he must do to help himself, he is taking an *active* stance toward his situation. This new perspective is contrary to the passive nature of depression, and is a vital step in the healing process.

In this chapter we will explore two active strategies for combating depression. Many people who suffer from depression have found that it is difficult to maintain depressing thoughts when they are engaged in physical exercise; depression and exercise seem to be incompatible. For this reason we believe that a book on depression would be incomplete without a discussion of the natural healing role of exercise. The last half of the chapter will be devoted to another natural element of health, nutrition and diet.

For centuries it has been known that a ''sound mind'' is related to a ''sound body.'' Good general health practices such as attention to a balanced diet, adequate sleep, and regular physical exercise clearly contribute to the maintenance of good physical, mental and spiritual health. Here again we see how much our body, mind and spirit are inter-related. In recent years the growing death rate from heart disease has stimulated public awareness of the importance of exercise and proper diet. ''Health foods'' and jogging have increased in popularity among people of all ages who are concerned about maintaining good health. Paralleling this interest among the general public has been a developing curiosity among medical and psychological researchers regarding the relationships between exercise, diet and depression. In the following pages we will examine some of their findings.

Exercise

A recent national survey[1] of over 1600 American adults revealed some very interesting findings concerning physical activity and overall well-being. Active people, especially those who engage in some form of physical exercise for more than 300 minutes per week, claim many health benefits such as feeling less tense, more relaxed, more disciplined, more productive, and able to enjoy a better sex life. They also report increased self-confidence, a better self-image, improved coordination, and increased stamina and strength. On a test of psychological well-being, 50% of highly active people (300+ minutes of exercise per week) scored positively as compared with 42% of less active people (150 minutes/ week), and 24% of inactive people (no vigorous physical activity at all). These findings support the conclusion reached by many individuals through their own personal experience with exercise.

Some current research reported by Dr. Otto Appenzeller of the University of New Mexico Medical School provides a clue as to how physical activity is related to emotional and psychological well-being. Dr. Appenzeller[2] found that the nervous system releases hormones called catecholamines (which are important neurotransmitters, discussed in Chapter VII) during marathon running. Catecholamines, known to be low in persons suffering from depression, were increased to levels of 600% above normal in all marathon runners studied in Dr. Appenzeller's research project. It seems reasonable to assume that this connection between running and depression-reducing hormones may be generalized to moderate forms of physical exercise. If this is so, as medical research studies seem to indicate, physical activity and fitness can serve a significant therapeutic role in the lives of people who suffer from depression.

In order to explore the possible healing value of exercise, several interesting experiments have been conducted recently with inactive, moderately depressed patients. In one such experimental study[3] a number of sedentary, depressed persons were invited to enter a guided, gradual program of running. These psychiatric patients experienced an almost immediate sense of relief from the symptoms of depression. They reported improved sleep, reduced tension, less sadness, and a renewed or new-found sense of well-being. Interestingly, this "running treatment" for depressed patients proved to be equal in effectiveness to a series of psychotherapy sessions which were received by another group of depressed patients in the treatment program.

Personal experience has clearly confirmed the great value of physical exercise. A number of years ago, I (Dick) injured my back when I fell from the roof of our home. As a result, I suffered with chronic and often acute back pain for several years. After unsuccessfully searching for relief through many different avenues of treatment, I discovered that physical exercise, especially brisk walking and moderate jogging, would often ease the discomfort and allow me to sleep somewhat more peacefully. During these years it occurred to friends with whom I shared in a small prayer group that the most effective healing ministry they could offer was to run with me at least four times weekly. This we did together for more than six months. My back gradually seemed to gain new strength and freedom from much of the severe pain I experienced in previous years.

We began our running project gradually and with caution. First of all, we resisted competitive running. Each of us began at different levels of fitness. While all of us enjoyed some significant improvement in and satisfaction with our health, each of us continued to maintain different levels of fitness. While running we took care to choose a pace so that all could converse easily together. Secondly, we experienced a growing mutual support which encouraged us to continue with the running program we had agreed upon. Those of us in our group who suffer from depression were pleasantly surprised to find that almost immediately our sense of well-being improved markedly as symptoms of depression were alleviated. Then as weeks passed we found that while running we were able to discuss and to pray about our lives in depth. Now and then one of us would be struck by an insight or inspiration which would prove most helpful. We always found it difficult if not impossible to sustain a ''depressing conversation'' while we were exercising. When exercise is carried out properly it seems to be directly opposed to negative or depressed thinking.

Exercise has become such a valued part of my life that I now continue with it independently, although I still enjoy the occasional company of friends while exercising. In addition to the physical benefits which have been great, I have found regular physical exercise to be a significant factor in my freedom from depression.

Why is physical exercise so helpful to some people in managing or overcoming depression? There are a number of reasons. Among them, as we have already discussed, is the increase in catecholamines, the anti-depression neurotransmitters produced by the nervous system during exercise. Research continues to explore the complicated biochemical aspects of depression, including the biochemical effects of exercise. Moderate physical activity, when it is done properly, is a natural, inherently pleasant activity. A regular increase in the number and quality of one's daily pleasant activities can be very helpful in relieving depression, as we discuss in detail in Chapters V and IX.

When one undertakes a program of regular exercise, particularly if one is not physically fit to begin with, a sense of success and mastery develops as one observes steady self-improvement. The patience and self-discipline which also develop along with the more physical attributes of strength, endurance and coordination are rewarding and increase one's self-image and confidence. The positive attitude engendered by exercise frequently generalizes to other activities as one learns that one *can* change oneself and one's lifestyle for the better. The many negative beliefs that begin "I can't . . ." are gradually undermined as a new, healthy lifestyle is cultivated. Because an exercise program is by its very nature active, it helps to counteract the passivity and helplessness so characteristic of depression. Exercise can become a positive "addiction" or habit which then can be consciously substituted for negative, neurotic habits and coping mechanisms. Physical activity also is therapeutic because it provides a healthy and reliable means of release for the emotional-physical elements of tension, anxiety and anger which often accompany depression. Also, exercise with its new and pleasurable bodily sensations of rhythm, movement, and a "good" feeling of fatigue and relaxation, serves as a distraction from annoying minor physical symptoms of depression. Without a doubt, there are very few medical and psychological treatments with as many advantages (and as few undesirable side effects) which are as inexpensive as regular physical exercise.

Psychiatrist John Greist and his colleagues at the University of Wisconsin Medical School emphasize some important cautions which may help to prevent or minimize the likelihood of injury, failure, an unpleasant experience, or giving up on an exercise program. First, before initiating any kind of exercise program, it is a good idea to check with one's physician. Although moderate exercise is rarely harmful for the average individual, it may be unwise for persons with special medical problems. Secondly, it is important to increase one's level of physical activity gradually and in line with one's growing physical capacity. When I (Chris) first began my running program, my physician insisted that I intersperse one block of brisk walking for every block of jogging. Over a period of several weeks I was gradually able to increase the total number of blocks I covered each evening. A third reminder is to be patient. If patience is ignored and you push yourself to accomplish too much too fast, the chances are great that you will become discouraged and abandon the exercise program. For this reason it is essential that one set realistic goals—goals that are high enough to allow one a sense of genuine satisfaction and accomplishment, but not so high that they are unreachable. To undertake an exercise program and then fail to meet one's unrealistic expectations can well leave one more depressed and less self-confident than before the exercise regimen was begun. Sensitivity to body signals can help one to set a realistic, moderate rate. Exercise should be paced so that breathing does not become so labored that it becomes difficult to talk with another person comfortably while exercising; also to be monitored are gait, footfall, balance, fatigue, and pain.

Lastly, if depressed thoughts intrude during one's exercise time, a conscious effort should be made to turn one's concentration to the physical aspects of what one is doing—to breathing, rhythm, or the sound and feeling of one's footfalls. Although exercising with others is more enjoyable for most people than exercising alone, it may be wise to avoid competition. As part of my exercise program I (Chris) resumed horseback riding lessons after an interval of many inactive years. Never having been athletically inclined and being quite out of shape physically, I was not doing as well with my lessons as were some of the others in the class. As I compared my meager progress with the performance of other students, I found that this part of my exercise program was increasing my depression rather than alleviating it. A friend helped me with this problem of secretly competing with others by suggesting that I praise myself for any and all progress that I made to level A to level B to level C—even if others had already arrived at level Z. I found that this positive mental attitude increased my enjoyment as I became more conscious of my own gradually growing mastery; the exercise program then became effective in helping me combat chronic depression.

Although much of the research regarding exercise for depression has been concerned with running, any form of physical activity can be used in an exercise plan for depression. Individual interests, abilities, and resources often determine what form of exercise one chooses: running, walking, swimming, dancing, bicycling, handball—there are many, many possibilities. Rhythmical activities such as walking, running, swimming and dancing, which are natural to human beings, are particularly helpful. One should select an activity which is personally pleasurable so that the exercise program does not become more work than play—although as with any self-help strategy for depression, determination and self-discipline are sometimes necessary to stay "with the program" when one is tired, despondent, or overwhelmed with other responsibilities.

In conclusion, research and experience reveal that a regular program of moderate exercise is helpful in relieving depression for many people. An active therapy, exercise uses self as a valuable health resource which helps to combat the passivity and helplessness so common in depression. Exercise contributes to general physical health by increasing cardio-pulmonary capacity and musculoskeletal strength. As a sense of mastery and achievement develops, one's self-concept is enhanced. Exercise promotes a healthy means of discharging anxiety, tension, and anger and promotes relaxation and a more realistic, optimistic view of one's self, one's situation, and one's world.

Nutrition

"You are what you eat," or so the saying goes. Although various authorities are in disagreement about some aspects of nutrition, none deny the importance of a diet that is balanced and wholesome and which includes the nutrients which are essential for health. Most people are aware of this relationship between nutrition and physical health. Poor nutrition inevitably results in vitamin deficiencies. As research and medical observation has shown, vitamin and other nutritional deficiencies may lead to depression, and/or a host of other emotional and physical problems. These in turn aggravate the problem even more by decreasing appetite. Because depression is so often accompanied by nutritional problems, this book would be incomplete without a brief examination of the relationship between diet and depression.

Often when one is depressed it is difficult to eat the things which are necessary for physical and mental health. Depression, particularly when it is severe, frequently is accompanied by anorexia, or loss of appetite. (Occasionally the reverse happens and the depressed person may increase his food intake and gain weight.) Friends and family members may become concerned as they helplessly stand by and watch their loved one shed pound after pound, unable to eat even minimal amounts of food. A friend who suffered from an acute depression described her struggle with food:

> Food tasted all the same and I did not care whether I ate cake or hamburger. I somehow knew that I had to eat in order to keep up a facade of "okay-ness." As my depression deepened I completely lost interest in food and stopped eating. The very thought of tasteless food

was nauseating. In a month's time I lost 30 pounds. My body shook; my legs were wobbly; I couldn't concentrate. Since I still had to provide for my children, I would go through grocery stores and reach for easy-to-prepare foods without daring to think about eating lest I become nauseated.

As her depression began to lift as a result of treatment with antidepressant medication, her appetite gradually returned and she eventually regained the weight she had lost during the depths of her illness.

With diet as with exercise, the interdependence of a sound mind and a sound body is clear. In this portion of the chapter we will investigate some nutritional topics related to depression. This relationship between nutrition and depression (and other mental disorders) has received increasing attention in recent years along with the growth of the orthomolecular school of psychiatry propounded by Nobel prize-winner Dr. Linus Pauling, Dr. David R. Hawkins, Dr. Abram Hoffer, and others.

Every function of the body depends upon nutrition. The nutrients contained in food we eat form the building blocks which the body uses for energy and for synthesis of the chemicals needed to maintain and repair the cells of the body. Through the complicated processes of digestion and metabolism, nutrients enter the bloodstream and from there go to every part of the body. The brain, which coordinates the mental and emotional life, requires many different nutrients to function. It can only receive those nutrients by means of the bloodstream. Thus if an essential nutrient is missing from the diet, the brain in some way suffers from that deficiency.

When the subject of nutrition and nutritional deficiency is brought up, a word which most often comes to mind is "vitamins." Vitamins are essential not just for health but for life itself. First discovered in 1911 by Dr. Casimir Funk of London who named them "vital-amines," vitamins are chemicals found in food and used by the body as enzymes and to make enzymes. Thus, vitamins are key elements that serve as triggers or catalysts for the many chemical reactions in our body, including the brain and nervous system. If there is a deficiency or an imbalance in the neurotransmitters at the nerve junctions, the nerve message is not communicated accurately or properly interpreted by the brain. Indeed, all of the message transmissions in the brain and nervous system depend in part upon a proper supply of vitamins and other nutrients.

While the body needs all the vitamins, it is the B-complex vitamins which are especially important for the maintenance and normal functioning of the brain and nervous system. When the body does not receive enough B vitamins every day, a variety of mental and emotional symptoms may develop. These symptoms may range from mild to severe, depending on how prolonged the deficiency is. Loss of appetite, irritability, confusion, memory loss, inability to concentrate, oversensitivity to noise, insomnia, nervousness, apprehensiveness, panic, and even hallucinations result from lack or deficiency of the B-complex vitamins in the diet. Depression and inability to tolerate stress are often early signs of deficiency.

Of course, moderate to severe vitamin deficiencies may have serious physical consequences as well, but we have listed the emotional, mental disturbances that may occur to show how essential vitamins are to sound mental health as well as to physical well-being. Pellagra, a potentially serious disease caused by niacin (Vitamin B3) deficiency, is characterized by fatigue, disorientation, depression, paranoia, skin rash, burning of the mucous membranes of the mouth and eyes, nausea, vomiting and diarrhea. Serious debility and even death may be the result unless the missing vitamins are added to the diet. Severe vitamin deficiency diseases such as pellagra are not limited only to Third World countries or the very poor! What everyone does not know is that it is not unusual even for middle class Americans to suffer from "hidden" malnutrition and vitamin deficiency. Early signs of vitamin deficiency are often emotional and mental—i.e., depression, inability to tolerate stress, nervousness, fatigue—which appear before serious physical illness develops. Depression and schizophrenia, in fact, are considered by some nutritionists to be early indications of pellagra.

The best assurance that adequate amounts of B vitamins are received by the brain and nervous system is a nutritionally balanced diet. The B-complex vitamins are found in a variety of foods, including whole grains, wheat germ, bran, Brewer's yeast, enriched cereals, liver and lean meat, fish, eggs, nuts, milk, and green leafy vegetables. Polished and refined flour and rice have had most or all B vitamins removed by the milling process. Overcooking can also destroy the B and C vitamins in food. Unlike the fat-soluble vitamins A, D, E and K, the B vitamins are water soluble, which means that the body uses what it needs of these vitamins each day and discards any excess. This protects the body from an accidental ''overdose'' of Vitamin B, but also means that an adequate amount of the B complex must be included in the diet every day. Vitamin C, another water-soluble vitamin found in fresh fruits and vegetables, must be taken in adequate amounts also, not only because Vitamin C is essential for health in its own right, but also because the B-complex vitamins cannot function properly in the body without Vitamin C. For the depressed person vitamins should be taken with the advice of the physician. While there is little danger of overdose with the water-soluble vitamins B and C, it is possible to damage the system by ingesting high dosages of the fat-soluble vitamins A, D, E and K. Vitamin pills never make up for an inadequate diet.

Before leaving the subject of vitamins, it should be noted that intake does not necessarily insure their absorption into the bloodstream. For reasons not clearly understood, some persons are unable to absorb adequate amounts of the B vitamins from the food they eat. In such cases the B-complex and C vitamins should be taken together by injection. Fortunately most people do not need to take their vitamins by injection. For those who suffer from depression, however, it may be wise to consult your physician about supplementing your dietary intake of Vitamin B and C with high potency oral vitamins available at any pharmacy or health store.

As we have seen, it is difficult to eat when one's appetite is diminished by depression. Although vitamin supplements cannot substitute for nutritious food, they can help to minimize the nutritional deficiencies which are likely to develop if regular meals are not eaten. Vitamins also have the added effect of increasing appetite in most persons. What must be avoided is to eliminate what little appetite remains with ''empty calories''—sugar or highly refined carbohydrates which have no nutritional value whatsoever. If one can only manage to eat a small amount of food, that food should be high in protein—meat, fish, dairy products, eggs, or legumes (lentils, soybeans, and similar beans). The body must have protein from which it makes serotonin and the catecholamines epinephrine and norepinephrine—the neurotransmitters in the brain and nervous system which must be kept in balance to avoid depression. Also, protein has the advantage that it can be transformed by the body into blood sugar for energy and other cell needs.

Another nutritional factor related to depression is the consumption of excessive amounts of refined sugar and starches (carbohydrates) in the diet. Americans consume massive amounts of sugar every day, sometimes without even realizing it. Sugar is added to many foods that we don't ordinarily think of as sweetened. For example, examine the labels of a variety of foods in your kitchen and discover how often sugar is listed as an added ingredient in such products as ketchup, chicken bouillon, salad dressing, barbeque sauce, bologna, peanut butter, soy sauce, various packaged seasonings, pickles and relish, even ordinary bread. In addition to the many hidden sources of refined sugar, many of us over-indulge in non-nutritional, vitamin-depleted, highly sweetened or processed foods such as pastries, ice cream, candy, soft drinks and others. Diabetes and obesity are not the only penalties for a high-sugar, high-carbohydrate diet. Depression may also be aggravated by excessive refined sugar and carbohydrates.

The principal energy source for the body is glucose sugar. Natural sugars such as the simple sugars in milk, fruit, and honey do not place as much strain on the body as refined sugars do. For example, sucrose or table sugar requires a complex response by the brain, pancreas, adrenal glands, and liver in order to be changed into usable glucose. The body is designed to maintain an optimum level of sugar in the blood. (No sugar in the blood is just as dangerous as too much sugar in the blood.) When refined sugar or carbohydrates are taken into the body they are quickly absorbed, causing the blood sugar level to rise suddenly. A regulating part of the brain called the hypothalamus reacts to this increased blood sugar by instructing the pancreas to secrete insulin into the bloodstream to decrease the level of sugar. But before the brain recognizes the blood sugar level has returned to normal and thus instructs the pancreas to stop pouring insulin into the bloodstream, too much insulin is secreted. This results in hypoglycemia, or *low* blood sugar. When this happens the person feels tired, light-headed, shaky, irritable, anxious, and depressed. Now the body responds by instructing the liver to convert stored sugar known as glycogen into glucose which finally raises the blood sugar level to normal. Every time we eat concentrated, refined sugar or carbohydrates, our body goes through this complex sequence of events in an attempt to deal with a substance that we were not designed to eat. Although we may feel that a candy bar or a bottle of soda pop gives us a quick boost of energy, the effect is only temporary because the outpouring of insulin which it triggers only drives the blood sugar even lower. Paradoxically, this in turn creates a craving for more sugar! Here is what happens:

REFINED SUGAR
and/or carbohydrates
are eaten

the BRAIN orders
the LIVER to convert
emergency reserves of
stored energy called
glycogen into glucose
to return blood sugar
to normal level

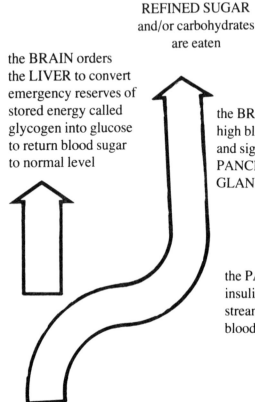

the BRAIN recognizes
high blood sugar level
and signals the
PANCREAS and ADRENAL
GLANDS

the PANCREAS secretes
insulin into the blood-
stream to lower the
blood sugar level

the body craves more
sugar or carbohydrates
in misguided attempt
to relieve "sugar
blues"

blood sugar plunges
BELOW NORMAL as too
much insulin is poured
into the blood

SUGAR BLUES:
depression, irrita-
bility, anxiousness,
shakiness, fatigue,
headache, etc. may be
experienced

If one continues to take in sugar, a new ''emergency'' response is begun before the old one has been resolved. This ''sugar seesaw'' means the body must work over-time in its efforts to maintain the delicate balance of blood sugar needed by the cells of the body. In the meantime, depression, confusion, and irritability are experienced.

With continued intake of refined sugars and carbohydrates, this regulating mechanism of the body can eventually become fatigued and malfunction. Hypoglycemia and/or diabetes may be the result. Because the cells of the brain and nervous system must have glucose (blood sugar) in order to carry out their normal functioning, any malfunction in the blood sugar level will almost surely produce emotional and mental symptoms, which frequently have been called the ''sugar blues'': depression, irritability, nervousness, disturbed concentration, fatigue, and inability to tolerate physical or mental stress. Hopefully the information about nutrition presented so far has reinforced the importance of a wholesome, balanced diet. Our total well-being depends upon it.

Exercise, Nutrition, and the Healing of Depression

The research on the biological causes of depression, together with what we have learned about the mental and emotional benefits of exercise and diet, strongly suggest that a lifestyle which is conducive to health is one which includes regular exercise and a balanced diet. Indeed, a ''sound mind *is* intimately related to a ''sound body.'' What we have advocated in this chapter is much more, we believe, than adherence to a passing health fad. Care for one's emotional and spiritual well-being requires equal care for one's body.

Clearly this chapter contains several implications for the healing of depression. In other chapters we have pictured the development and maintenance of depression as a function of negative thinking, withdrawal, and helplessness. Here we can now *reverse* sequence to illustrate healing based on a lifestyle which includes regular exercise and a balanced diet.

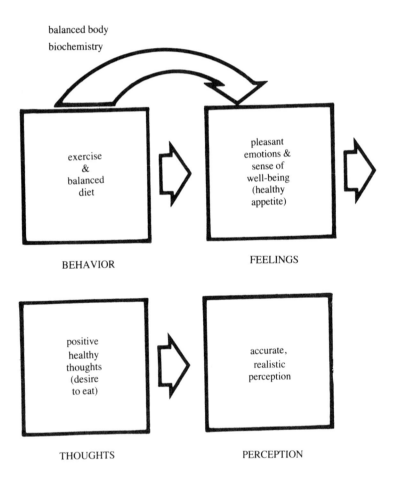

A New Kind of Fasting

In advocating a holistic approach to healing throughout this book we affirm our conviction that wholeness and holiness depend upon a body, mind, and spirit which are in harmony with one another. The contents of this chapter dealing with exercise and diet suggest the need for a disciplined life, the focus of which is the achievement of health and wholeness. In a sense this disciplined life entails a new kind of fasting, not unlike that spoken of by Isaiah the prophet:

Is not this the sort of fast that pleases me
—it is the Lord Yahweh who speaks—
to break unjust fetters
and undo the thongs of the yoke,

to let the oppressed go free,
and break every yoke,
to share your bread with the hungry,
and shelter the homeless poor,

to clothe the man you see to be naked
and not turn from your own kin?
Then will your light shine like the dawn
and your wound be quickly healed over. . . .

If you do away with the yoke,
the clenched fist, the wicked word,
if you give your bread to the hungry,
and relief to the oppressed,

your light will rise in the darkness,
and your shadows become like noon.
Yahweh will always guide you,
giving you relief in desert places.

He will give strength to your bones,
and you shall be like a watered garden,
like a spring water
whose waters never run dry (Is 58:6-11).

In Isaiah chapter 58 we read about a new kind of fasting, true fasting that is pleasing to the Lord and healing to mankind. This discipline of the heart and of the hands is more than a mere abstinence from food, drink and activity. It is a way of life by which we open our heart to the Word of God and to others. For the Old Testament Jews to whom the prophet Isaiah spoke, this was a revolutionary message: it was a call to penetrate beyond external ritual observances to the very heart of the commandments and to discover their true significance. What Yahweh was trying to tell Israel (and us, too) was that the greatest worship that one may offer Him is not to be miserable but to be bearers of comfort, freedom, and justice. Jesus said that what he desires is mercy, not sacrifice (Mt 9:13).

What this reflection suggests for one who suffers from depression is a new way of life. It emphasizes not a literal fasting from nourishing food and healthful exercise, but a new desire to be whole and to share this wholeness with others. One of the spiritual benefits of traditional fasting is that it allows one to undertake, willingly, a sacrificial form of self-discipline which is pleasing to God and beneficial to neighbor. In the same way, the self-discipline of physical exercise and nutritious diet is a parallel form of "fasting" for the depressed person. In so doing, one may help to "let the oppressed go free and break every yoke."

Footnotes

1. Jane E. Brody, "Fitness Poll Yields Some Surprises," *New York Times*, 29 January 1979, p. C9.
2. Otto Appenzeller and David R. Schade, "Neurology of Endurance Training. Sympathetic Activity During a Marathon Race," Paper presented at the 1979 Meeting of the American Academy of Neurology.
3. John H. Greist, Marjorie H. Klein, Roger R. Eischens, John Faris, Alan S. Gurman, and William P. Morgan, "Running as Treatment for Depression," *Comprehensive Psychiatry*, 20, (1979), 44-54.

CHAPTER NINE

PSYCHOLOGICAL SELF-HELP STRATEGIES

In Chapters IV and V we examined the role played by our thoughts and our activities—or rather our *irrational* thinking and our *withdrawal* from activities—in creating and maintaining depression. Becoming *aware* of the thoughts and behaviors which contribute to feelings of depression is an essential first step in bringing about change. The notion of changing one's ways of thinking and responding may seem a little overwhelming. Can one really change patterns which have become well-established habits with years of practice? The answer to this question is definitely ''Yes!'' The key to change is to take it step by step; once the process is broken down into manageable pieces, which can be tackled one at a time, the task of self-change no longer appears so impossible. In Chapter II we used the image of the depressed person being trapped in a deep pit, and we spoke of the need for a ladder by which one may climb up and out of the pit. The exercises which are described on the following pages may help to serve as rungs on such a ladder out of the pit of depression.

It is helpful to read about the dynamics and causes of depression, but there is no good substitute for the insight that comes when one is able to discover, first-hand, the patterns of one's own life which lead to depression. Because each person's past experiences, thought habits, and behavior patterns are unique, no book can tell you exactly what needs changing in *your* life. That is something which only *you* can discover. Often the process of psychotherapy can assist people in recognizing and then changing areas of difficulty in their lives. More and more psychotherapists are recommending exercises just like the ones in this chapter because they have proven effective in helping people to overcome depression. These exercises are designed to assist *you* in discovering and then changing the unique factors in *your* life which are helping to create and maintain depression-producing feelings and lifestyle.

This chapter encourages you to get personally, directly involved in the change/healing process. To be effective these exercises will require you to invest a small amount of time and effort on a daily basis. Experience has shown that 15 or 20 minutes at the end of each day is sufficient, and many depressed people have found that the information they have gained about themselves and their depression has made this modest investment well worthwhile. You may not feel that you can or want to utilize the exercises in this chapter. Some people are not attracted to an active, "workbook" approach to healing. If you are convinced this is true of you, you may want to skip this chapter and go on to Chapter X. Before you decide to do that, however, we strongly encourage you to give this approach a try. Most people who have done so have discovered that these self-change projects were not only interesting and revealing but also helped to stimulate significant changes in the thought and behavior habits which were contributing to their depression. As you read on, you will find that the exercises presented in this chapter are not difficult.

EXERCISE I: A STRATEGY FOR OVERCOMING DEPRESSED THINKING

Our feelings, as we discussed in Chapter IV, do not just "happen." How we feel, and consequently our behavior, is directly connected to what we *think*. Likewise, our thinking is stimulated by our perception of some event. This is the sequence:

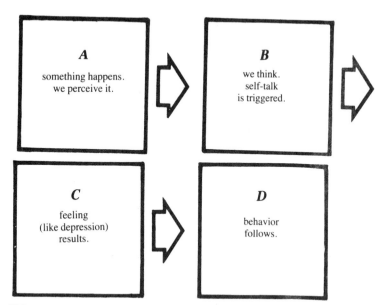

We are going to begin by attacking this depression sequence at Block B, self-talk based on our belief system. Irrational beliefs and the illogical and distorted things we unintentionally tell ourselves were learned very early in life. These ingrained patterns continue largely because they are rarely if ever challenged. Irrational thinking which leads to depression is a deeply entrenched personal habit which, like all other habits, is strengthened each time it is repeated. Any habit which has become so automatic and firmly established will not ordinarily disappear overnight. *But it can be conquered!* With persistent and vigorous effort, we can learn to overcome the thought patterns which create and sustain depression.

Developing new, rational beliefs to replace our basically unrealistic ideas and negative self-talk will help to build good feelings and healthy, appropriate behavior. Psychologists and psychiatrists, notably Dr. Albert Ellis and Dr. Aaron Beck, have proposed a number of methods to help accomplish the goal of healthy, rational thinking.

STEP ONE: Identifying Self-Talk

The initial step in changing irrational or distorted thought patterns is to identify the depression-producing self-talk and the kinds of events which trigger it. A method which has proven helpful for many depressed people is a journal. The journal is a tool which can be effectively used to make one aware of the depression sequence in one's life.

Every day, record at least one sequence in your journal like this (for now, ignore Column D):

Date	A. Event	B. Self-Talk	C. Feeling	D. Dispute
9/20	Lost my temper with the kids	"I shouldn't ever yell at the children; I'm a terrible mother."	Depression	
9/21	Forgot an appointment with a friend	"Jim must really be annoyed with me. I'm sure he thinks I am mad at him and thinks I intentionally stood him up."	Worried & Guilty	
9/22	Attempted to pray	"God is angry with me or He wouldn't be leaving me feeling so abandoned and unconsoled. This is a sure sign that I'm unforgivably bad; even God has given up on me."	Emptiness, Doubt, and Guilt	

Begin by recalling an unpleasant emotion or feeling you experienced during the day, and record it in Column C. Describe it simply: sad, disgusted, hurt, angry, shut out, empty, guilty, depressed, etc. Then in Column A briefly jot down the event or situation which preceded and seemed to trigger the unpleasant feeling. Now try to remember the kinds of things you said to yourself at the time. What was your self-talk? Good clues to negative self-talk are words like "should," "must," "terrible," "awful," "I can't," and labels such as "stupid," "no good," "loser," etc. (It may be helpful to review Chapter IV in which the characteristics of negative thoughts were described.) List your self-talk as accurately as you can in Column B.

At first you may find it difficult to remember "A-B-C sequences." As you do this day by day, however, it will become easier because now you are on the alert. You will become increasingly more aware of your self-talk and the kinds of situations which most often trigger feelings of depression. *A major goal of these exercises is to facilitate this awareness.* Once you begin to recognize the events and thoughts which are linked to unpleasant feelings of guilt, worthlessness and depression, you can begin to *actively change how you feel.* This is the goal of Step Two.

STEP TWO: *Disputing Irrational Self-Talk*

Any enemy possesses more power while it remains hidden than it does when it is exposed and visible. This same principle applies to depression-producing thinking habits. The more automatic and unnoticed our negative thoughts and irrational beliefs are, the greater their influence on us becomes. Thus, by working to make these thoughts conscious, we have taken a very important first step in breaking their power over us.

There are many things which happen to us in our daily lives over which we have no control. For example, it is no one's fault if it rains on the Fourth of July. Some people quickly adjust to the circumstances by making new plans to celebrate the holiday indoors. On the other hand, there will be other persons who become depressed, believing their holiday plans to be irreparably ruined by the unwelcome bad weather. We could picture these two different responses and their consequences like this:

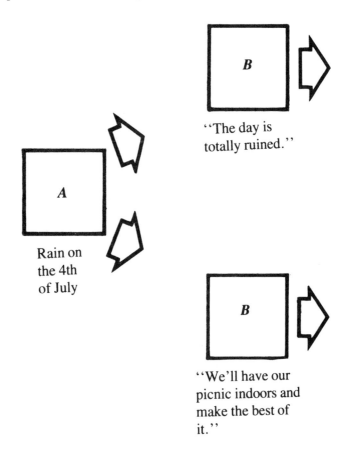

"The day is totally ruined."

Rain on the 4th of July

"We'll have our picnic indoors and make the best of it."

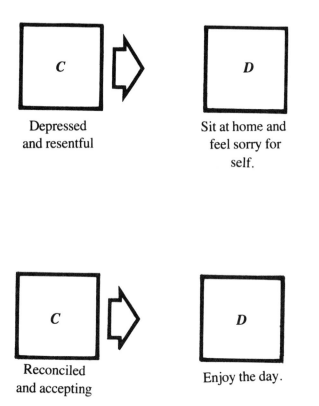

The outcome for each is very different although in both sequences the precipitating event—the rainy weather—is the same. The difference is a direct result of the thoughts and assumptions one has in response to the event.

We often cannot choose the circumstances or events in our lives; however, we *can* choose how we will respond to them. For any given event in our daily lives there are many possible responses, i.e., thoughts and consequent feelings and behavior. These responses range all the way from those which are very rational, logical and realistic to those which are just the opposite—irrational, distorted, inappropriate, and unhealthy. As we discovered in Chapter IV, a major problem among persons who suffer from depression is that their irrational beliefs and negative self-talk (i.e., "The day is totally ruined." outnumber and overpower those which are reasonable (i.e., "We'll have our picnic indoors and make the best of it."). In other words, one's situation seems filled with problems instead of opportunities when one is depressed.

Having identified one's negative and irrational self-talk in Step One, the next step is to learn to "counter" or dispute one's self-talk. When we dispute our irrational self-talk, we logically examine it and then "counter" it with reasonable, healthy thoughts. As you study your self-talk, ask yourself questions such as these:

* Can I *rationally* support this belief?
* What *evidence* is there that this is true? Is there evidence that this is false?
* What is the worst thing that could happen even if this *is* true?
* *Why* should I? (For "shoulds," "musts," and "oughts," always ask *Why?*)

It is often difficult for a depressed person to come up with anything but more negative responses to these questions, so firmly is he bound by his habit of thinking negatively. A friend can be a real help here. You may want to enlist the assistance of a trusted friend who can help you to dispute your negative self-talk.

Returning to the journal entry illustrated in Step One, we are ready to fill in Column D:

Date	A. Event	B. Self-Talk	C. Feeling	D. Dispute
9/20	Lost my temper with the kids	"I shouldn't ever yell at the children; I'm a terrible mother."	Depressed	It's only human to express anger at times; besides, I know I'm a good mother.
9/21	Forgot an appointment with a friend	"Jim must really be annoyed with me. I'm sure he thinks I am mad at him and thinks I intentionally stood him up."	Worried & Guilty	Jim has known me too long and is too good a friend to think I would have done this intentionally. I'll call him in the morning and explain, and Jim will understand.
9/22	Attempted to pray	"God is angry with me or He wouldn't be leaving me feeling so abandoned and unconsoled. This is a sure sign that I'm unforgivably bad; even God has given up on me."	Empty, Guilty, & full of Doubts	God has promised in the scriptures that He will never abandon me. I know that my feelings can't be trusted when I'm depressed. Just because I don't feel His loving presence doesn't mean He does not love me.

For every event or situation, there are many possible responses. The objective of this exercise is to stop and think of alternative, *realistic* responses to the habitually negative thinking of depression. Using the journal to record one event-thought-feeling-dispute sequence daily will facilitate awareness of thought patterns and will begin to establish a new, healthy habit of realistic thinking. Because feelings follow thoughts, depression will be decreased as negative, irrational thinking is replaced by realistic thinking.

For an in-depth and very readable presentation of the relationship between thoughts and feelings, plus clear, point-by-point directions for disputing irrational beliefs, the reader is referred to *A New Guide to Rational Living* by Albert Ellis and Robert Harper (No. Hollywood, California: Wilshire Book Co., 1977). If unavailable from your local bookseller, this and other related publications may be obtained by writing the Institute for Rational Living, Inc., 45 East 65th Street, New York, New York 10021.

EXERCISE II: THE DEPRESSION-ACTIVITY CONNECTION

If a persistent support for depression is too many negative experiences and not enough positive activities in one's life, then a primary goal for overcoming depression is to restore the missing balance of pleasant experiences. We can begin to do this by evaluating the type, quality and effect of our relationships and activities. Before we can change, we must know just what needs changing. The purpose of the following exercise is to help you look carefully at your life, especially your interactions with others and your activities. You will need to identify which particular relationships and activities lead to positive ''pay-offs'' for you and which ones produce negative feelings and depression-fostering behavior.

Dr. Peter Lewinsohn[1] has developed a simple system that you can use to help identify the positives and negatives in your life. This requires some detective work! Here's how to do it.

STEP ONE: Rating Your Mood

Keeping track of your mood variations from day to day has several useful purposes. It will be particularly helpful to you in your detective work of identifying the events and situations which usually make you feel good and those which often make you feel bad. It will also help you to evaluate your progress from day to day. This is easy to do once you make it a habit.

Although it often seems so, no one is depressed *all* of the time. Take a moment and think back over today. Was this a good day for you, in which you felt relatively content and happy? Or were you really depressed today? On a scale of 1 to 9, rate your mood for the day. A "9" means that you felt really terrific; a "1" would mean you hit rock bottom and were as depressed as you can ever imagine yourself feeling. Many times you will find yourself somewhere in between these two extremes.

STEP TWO: Counting Pleasant Events

A daily review of the activities, events and relationships in your life which make you feel good will help you to identify those kinds of things which you want to *increase* in order to get yourself out of the vicious cycle of depression. Every evening before you go to bed, at the same time you rate your mood (Step One), take a few minutes to reflect back over your day. To help you recall pleasant events, a list of typical pleasant experiences is provided on page 144. (If you did an activity or experienced an event on the list but did not feel it was pleasant or enjoyable for *you*, then do not count it when you count your "Pleasant Events." The list is only a guide.) You may have had pleasant experiences which are not included on the list. This list (and the one in Step Three) are meant to serve only as helps to you in recalling and counting the pleasant events in your own life. It is *not* intended to be a list of things which we are suggesting you "should" or "ought" to be doing. It is merely a personal checklist to help you assess the role your experiences play in maintaining feelings of depression. The items on the list are ones which we believe many people commonly experience. This review won't take long, especially after you have done it a few times.

STEP TWO: DAILY PLEASANT EVENTS CHECKLIST

Being in good health
Thinking about people I like
Feeling the presence of the Lord in my life
Sleeping soundly at night
Receiving a gift
Enjoying children
Planning a trip or special occasion
Experiencing peace and quiet
Having a frank & open conversation
Being complimented or told I have done well
Being told I am appreciated or loved
Learning to do something new
Enjoying good food
Knowing I look nice
Saying something clearly
Worshipping God
Laughing
Enjoying a novel, movie, concert, play, etc.
Enjoying the effects of physical exercise
Thinking about something good in the future
Accomplishing a task or meeting a goal
Enjoying spare time
Wearing clean, comfortable clothes
Being pleasantly surprised
Seeing good things happen to my family or friends
Seeing beautiful scenery
Having sexual relations
Doing a job well
Being with friends
Doing something to help someone else
Getting good news
Being nice to myself in some way

Spending time on an enjoyable project or hobby
Playing fun games
Taking some time or a day off

STEP THREE: *Counting Unpleasant Events*

Next, think back over your day and try to recall the unpleasant events which you experienced. The list below may help you in making this inventory.

STEP THREE: DAILY UNPLEASANT EVENTS CHECKLIST

Hearing bad news
Worrying about the future
Being misunderstood or misquoted
Making a bad decision/knowing I am in the wrong
Leaving a task uncompleted/procrastinating
Having someone disagree with me
Having someone criticize me
Arguing with spouse, family member, or friend
Knowing that someone I care about is unhappy, sick, etc.
Performing poorly in sports, on the job, school, etc.
Doing something I don't want to do in order to please someone else
Being late
Declining to help or to respond to someone
Feeling empty and confused
Being exhausted
Having too much to do
Failing at something
Being bored
Being unable to solve a dilemma
Working under too much pressure
Feeling overwhelmed by sin or guilt feelings

Realizing I can't do what I had thought or hoped I could
Being in a noisy, crowded, dirty, or messy place
Working on something when I am tired
Being near unpleasant people (drunk, inconsiderate, etc.)
Realizing that someone I love and I are growing apart
Being without privacy
Being physically uncomfortable (sick, headachy, cold, etc.)
Bad weather
Having financial worries
Being sexually frustrated
Being alone when I'd prefer to be with others
Being frustrated with my spiritual life

STEP FOUR: Comparing Your Mood with Daily Events

The purpose of this step is to have you see clearly just how much your mood is affected by your daily experiences. Most people who have done this exercise have discovered that almost always, when their day has been filled with a large number of unpleasant events and a correspondingly low number of pleasant experiences, they will have rated their mood toward the "depressed" end of the mood scale.

Compare your mood rating with the number of pleasant and unpleasant events which you experienced during the day. You may find it helpful to keep a daily record of your mood rating and the number of pleasant events and unpleasant events. Some people find that plotting these on a graph is especially helpful in visualizing just how much daily experiences affect mood.

It will take more than one week to get a good idea of what is happening, so don't jump to any immediate conclusions. After about two weeks, however, you will begin to see a pattern. You will probably discover that the number of Unpleasant Events is greatest on days when you felt your worst. On days when you are feeling pretty good, you most likely will have experienced a large number of Pleasant Activities. When your Pleasant Activities go up, your mood rating goes up, too.

It is very important that you take the time to go through these simple exercises. Each day it will become a bit easier. As time passes you will find that you are becoming more and more alert to your activities and relationships during the course of a day and the effect these activities and relationships have on how you feel and respond. These simple "homework" procedures help you to become aware of how much *what you do affects how you feel.* Soon you will begin to feel better because you are more alert to your activities, thoughts, and feelings, and you are taking positive action to counteract your depression. You are no longer helpless!

EXERCISE III: PINPOINTING PROBLEM AREAS

In the case of depression, many times events, thoughts or feelings come before and discourage or block us from doing something or enjoying what we *actually* do. In other words, when we look for these antecedents we are really looking for the *reasons* for a low number of pleasant experiences. *Why* aren't we doing as many of the enjoyable things we used to do before we became depressed? And why do we get so little enjoyment from those things that we *actually* do?

STEP ONE: Recognizing Antecedents

To help pinpoint these antecedent causes, ask yourself questions like these (the information from Exercises I and II will help you out here):

* Do I usually feel worse at a particular time of day?

* If so, what happens (or doesn't happen) at that particular time which might be making me feel low? (For instance, are you particularly depressed late in the evening when things are quiet at home and you are alone with your thoughts and have time to ruminate over your troubles?

* Do I often feel "down" when I'm with a particular person? (Maybe you have a certain friend who seems to drag you down; or maybe certain individuals allow or encourage you to "talk depression" when you are together.)

* Is any particular pastime (such as watching television) frequently associated with "down" times for you?

* What kinds of things do you say to yourself that have the effect of discouraging you? (your negative self-talk, e.g., "My friends think I'm dumb," "I'll never be able to do this right," "I'm losing my mind and there's nothing I can do about it," "God has abandoned me," etc. Refer back to Exercise I).

The answers to these kinds of questions will be very important to you in planning your anti-depression tactics.

"This whole thing is ridiculous," you may be saying to yourself. "I don't do much anymore *because* I am so depressed." Or are you depressed because you aren't doing anything pleasant? Which is the cause and which the effect? This is a classic "Which-came-first-the chicken-or-the-egg?" question. It works like this:

The answer isn't really important. We know that the two are very much related. When one is changed, the other will change also. When you increase your pleasant experiences you will feel less depressed. And when your depression lifts you will feel more like being active.

But back to the question of *Why*. Dr. Lewinsohn and his colleagues[2] have identified four common reasons why people have too few pleasant experiences in their daily lives. They are worth going over because they may apply to you. When you read them think about your own experiences:

1. Pressure from activities which are not pleasant but which must be performed.

For example, housework, caring for the children, writing a term paper, taking the bus back and forth to work everyday, attending boring but necessary meetings, etc. There are many things that have to be done but which are not particularly enjoyable. In coping with this problem it may be helpful to make yourself a simple time schedule in which you make sure to budget time for yourself (the things you want to do and enjoy doing) in addition to the responsibilities which must be done.

2. Lack of care in choosing activities with high pleasantness potential.

Quality can often compensate for quantity. If your time and resources are limited (as they are for most of us), give extra care to selecting activities which yield the greatest enjoyment and satisfaction.

3. Many major changes in a person's life situation may remove the availability of formerly very reinforcing activities.

This is what happens, for instance, at retirement; the same thing happens to a wife and mother when her children grow up and leave home and seemingly don't need her anymore. The need here is to reinvest your energy into new activities and relationships which may replace those which are no longer available to you.

4. Anxiety and discomfort interfere with enjoyment.

This is especially true for shy persons who find social activities painful. The shy person can learn to be more comfortable in social situations by focusing on others and their interests and needs and not on himself or what he believes others are thinking about him. Much of the discomfort experienced by the shy, introverted person is a result of his poor self-concept which leads him to irrationally conclude that others are observing him and noting his supposed unattractiveness, incompetence, clumsiness, or lack of intelligence. By turning his attention outward to others, he not only cultivates the arts of listening and caring for others, but he enjoys himself and others more. As we have already seen, our friendships and interactions with others are powerful, essential sources of reinforcement. The dilemma is whether to endure the initial anxiety that comes with learning new social skills or to withdraw into isolation and depression.

Learning to relax to counteract tension can also be very helpful when anxiety is a major problem. It seems to be an unfortunate fact of life that we often experience some short-term discomfort before we are able to enjoy the long-term benefits of healing and freedom. There will be times when we will find it necessary to do something which creates initial anxiety; here is the fork in the road to healing where we must choose to either turn back or to forge ahead, with courage and with faith, on our way to growth and happiness.

STEP TWO: Make A Plan and Follow It

Now that you have collected some data, you should have a pretty good idea about what your particular problem areas are. For instance, if your record-keeping reveals that your pleasant events (along with your mood) drastically decrease on weekends, then you know that planning more activities for Saturdays and Sundays is a high priority for you. In planning, concentrate on these kinds of experiences:

* Social interactions in which you feel wanted, liked, respected, understood, appreciated, accepted, and loved.

* Activities associated with feelings of adequacy, competence, independence, and purpose.

* Activities which are naturally pleasant (eating, laughing, seeing beautiful scenery, etc.).

Dr. Lewinsohn's research has shown that when people engage in these particular types of experiences they feel good, and when they do not have many of these kinds of experiences they tend to feel more depressed. These are clearly mood-related activities and provide some clues as to the kind of activities you will want to concentrate on adding to your daily schedule.

Plan a daily schedule for yourself, being sure to include especially those activities that will involve you in pleasant and meaningful interactions and relationships with others. Choose activities which you have found usually make you feel capable, talented and worthwhile. Make it a point to specifically plan some extra-enjoyable activities which perhaps you have avoided since you became depressed. Since there is a strong temptation to withdraw from contact with others when one is depressed, resist this tendency by limiting the number of solitary activities you will allow yourself (such as reading, watching television, etc.).

Keep your plan realistic; don't try to squeeze more into your day than you can realistically handle (but be sure not to leave large gaps of "empty" time which you will end up filling in with "depression-thinking"). Also, over-scheduling may create feelings of worry and guilt if you can't follow through with your schedule. Go easy on yourself when you fall off your plan, but promise yourself that you will work harder at it tomorrow. As you go through the week you will perhaps discover that some changes need to be made in your plan so that it will be more efficient and manageable. Don't be afraid to make changes when necessary, but beware of talking yourself out of activities in order to withdraw and indulge your depression!

For an in-depth and very readable presentation of this kind of active approach to the healing of depression, the reader is strongly encouraged to refer to *Control Your Depression* by Peter M. Lewinsohn, Ricardo F. Munoz, Mary Ann Youngren and Antoinette M. Zeiss (Prentice-Hall, 1978, $6.95 paperback).

Each person's ladder out of the pit of depression will be different, for the fundamental reason that each person is unique. Personal background, interests, abilities, family life, and resources are all very individual matters. That is why the exercises in this chapter and the anti-depression plans which may grow out of them constitute a very personal and unique project which can be conveniently structured to fit any situation or way of life. These psychological self-help strategies, together with the physical and spiritual avenues of healing, can be powerfully effective in bringing about lasting relief from the darkness and pain of depression.

Footnotes

1. Peter M. Lewinsohn *et al.*, *Control Your Depression* (Englewood Cliffs, N.J.: Prentice-Hall, Inc., 1978).
2. Lewinsohn *et al.*, pp. 154-156.

CHAPTER TEN

THE SPIRITUAL HEALING OF DEPRESSION

Proclaim with me the greatness of the Lord, together let us extol his name. I seek the Lord, and he answers me and frees me from all my fears. Every face turned to him grows brighter and is never ashamed. A cry goes up from the poor man, and the Lord hears and helps him in all his troubles. The Lord is near to the brokenhearted, he helps those whose spirit is crushed (Ps 34:3-6, 18).

One hot summer afternoon in Texas my telephone rang. When I (Dick) answered it I was surprised to hear the voice of a long-time friend. Marie, her sadness readily apparent in her voice, briefly told me she was in trouble; could I come and see her? After telling her I would be there a little later, I quickly telephoned my friend Alice and arranged for her to join me. When Marie answered the door we were taken aback by her appearance: her face was tear-stained and drooped as though burdened by a heavy weight. The three of us sat down to talk and little by little her story emerged.

Marie was a woman in her 50's, the wife of a prominent corporation executive. She had been hospitalized twice in the past for reactive depression, and she was once again sliding rapidly into the slough of depression. As before, her depression was precipitated by a definite event in her life. A few weeks ago her son George was arrested for embezzling a sizable amount of money from the firm for which he worked as chief accountant. His crime had received considerable publicity in the newspapers and in the local business community within which Marie and her husband were professionally and socially active. Marie felt that George had humiliated the family name and held them all up for public ridicule and contempt. Consumed with bitterness, anger and resentment, Marie accused George's wife of instigating the theft. She called all of the family members to express her abhorrence of George's action, and further, blamed them all for not somehow preventing this disgrace which had fallen upon the family. Over the weeks depression began to develop. Physically weak and emotionally exhausted, Marie became unable to go about her normal affairs. Ashamed and afraid of meeting friends or acquaintances at the grocery store, she refused to leave the house; now her cupboards were bare and there was no food in the house to eat. A deep, heartfelt sadness even smothered her attempts to pray. Depression was making itself felt in her spiritual life as a paralyzing sadness. She knew that things had gotten out of control, and decided she must ask for help.

As Alice and I listened to her, a single fact continually remained prominent: Marie was filled with resentment. Again and again she returned to the subject of her bitterness toward her son for shaming the family. She said she could not understand or forgive what he had done. There was no doubt in my mind that resentment was Marie's key problem. (Interestingly, Marie's husband recognized that her depression was related to George's misdeeds, and he actually encouraged her sense of outrage and resentment. He could not see that it was not George's behavior which was making Marie sick, but it was Marie's resentment and refusal to forgive which had plunged her into depression.) A passage from the Gospel of Mark came strongly to Alice's mind, and she opened her New Testament and read it aloud to us:

And when you stand in prayer, forgive whatever you have against anybody, so that your Father in heaven may forgive your failings, too (Mk 11:25).

Marie listened intently, then asked Alice to read it once more. She felt it perhaps held a clue to her healing. After prayerfully going over it a third time, Marie became convinced that she must take the scripture literally. The words of Jesus left no loopholes: "You must forgive *anything* you have against *anybody.*" She decided at that moment that she must call all of her relatives and ask their forgiveness for her unkind words of anger and blame. This was clearly a good beginning. I asked her then if she was willing to forgive George. She thought for awhile, then answered hesitatingly, "No . . . I can't forgive him, at least not without God's help." We prayed then with her that God would give her the grace she needed to forgive. Slowly Marie's face changed; the mental confusion and the sagging expression on her face lifted. She appeared happy and almost peaceful.

A few years later when I visited her in Texas, Marie told me that that night she felt as though a stone had been lifted from her heart. Her depression dissipated gradually as she was able to let go of her resentment and refusal to forgive. For Marie the healing of depression was intimately connected to a spiritual problem. To become free of her sadness she had to be willing to forgive; for this she needed the help of trusted friends and, of course, a loving, healing Lord. Marie continues to know and practice forgiveness, and for her this has been an essential element in her continuing freedom from severe depression.

Marie's story is important, because it demonstrates in a striking way how the emotional and spiritual effects of resentment are related to depression. Resentment, with its gripping anger and lingering hatred, is nearly instinctive or "automatic" for most of us. When resentments have "free run in our heart," even when they are as ingrained as scarcely-noticed habits, we can usually expect to experience the unwelcome manifestations of depression in our spiritual life called sadness. It is as if sadness is a tree nourished through roots of unforgiveness deeply embedded in our past lives, in our memories.

The Roots of Unforgiveness

Each one of us is formed by what we experience in life: by memories of our past, by present events, and by our own unique individual response to those memories and events. Although in previous chapters we have emphasized the role of the perceptions, thought patterns, and behaviors which occur largely in the here-and-now, depression also has roots in memories of the past—some recalled, others long forgotten. The experiences of our childhood have a deep and lasting effect on how we see ourselves, others, and God. In considering the focus and methods of the spiritual healing of depression and its sadness, it will be helpful to examine carefully some of the basic, common patterns of development which are shared by many persons who suffer from depression. From this "early life history" review may come insights into areas in need of healing that are specifically spiritual.

In infancy the child is totally dependent upon mother for his physical and emotional survival. It is mother (or in some cases, another primary person) who provides the infant nourishment, warmth, cleansing, and the gentle handling which clearly signal love and security. Thus it is at this very young age that the little person learns to trust others. During the infant's day full of needs, frustrations, cries and happiness, mother is known to be loving, even if not always responsive, and this creates the child's basic trusting stance which develops during his life. Trust is fostered by mothering which is experienced as faithful.

Sometimes the infant's experiences with mother are predominantly unstable and frustrating. When the child's cries for attention and care are almost always responded to with irritation or repeatedly ignored, the child learns that mother and others cannot be trusted. The baby begins to *feel* what it means to be unappreciated and neglected but he does not understand the reason for these feelings or why this is happening to him. All he knows is that he arrived into an unwelcoming, unloving world. A start in life like this soon teaches the little person basic mistrust of others who will be immediately perceived as unreliable and unfaithful.

Psychologists acknowledge that such early experiences develop a low tolerance for frustration in the infant. When mother or others fail to respond to the infant's needs, the child becomes "automatically" and unreasonably angry or frustrated. It is this basic experience with mistrust which often predisposes the child to the development of depression later in life. Although almost always unconscious, strong feelings of resentment and hostility are germinated and rooted in these early months of life. This resentment contains the seeds of withholding forgiveness from others and self. Without knowing why these feelings are so strong, the child concludes "I am not loved," and in his frustration and resentment seems unable to forgive others for his unhappy condition.

Janet, a young wife and mother, came to me (Chris) because she was chronically depressed. She was convinced deep down that she was an unloved and unwanted person. Janet's inability to accept the love of others was creating difficulties in her marriage; she also was deeply concerned that she was unable to provide her children with the devotion and love she wanted them to experience. I talked with her for awhile and as Janet gradually uncovered some long-forgotten memories of her childhood, she began to cry. Janet had been an unwanted baby. With a brother and sister who were one and two years older than she, she was seen as an unwelcome burden by her mother. At a young age her mother told her of how she had tried to give her away to the doctors and nurses in the delivery room; she wanted neither to see nor to hold her newborn daughter. For reasons that were not at all clear, Janet's mother reminded her over the years of how she had tried to give her away but how no one wanted her. The result of this knowledge was a child who grew up feeling and believing that not even mother could be counted on to provide love and security; those closest to her could not be trusted. With a forcefulness which she had not known existed within her, this young woman poured out with tears a story of lifelong resentment and deep, deep inner pain. We prayed together, and after awhile I suggested she use her faith-imagination to invite Jesus into that scene of rejection so many years ago in the hospital delivery room. I sat with her quietly, and in a few moments the tears again began to stream down her cheeks, only this time Janet was smiling and the tears signified the new peace which was filling her. She then told me that she visualized herself being born into the loving, receptive hands of Jesus. As he took her in his arms and held her to his heart, Janet experienced for the first time the reality of being treasured and loved. She then imagined Jesus told her that for all eternity he had looked forward to the day of her birth when she would become a part of his family. Gone was the pain of her mother's rejection as the Lord began to heal the wound created by Janet's painful memories. We then talked about her need to forgive her mother. Over the weeks and months which followed this initial healing encounter, she found that her willingness to forgive her mother and to let go of her long-standing resentments had to be renewed from time to time. The total process of healing, while well begun on that day of our prayer together, has taken time to fully develop in her life. Today Janet is largely free of the crippling effects of that early maternal rejection and the mistrust, resentment, and attitude of unforgiveness which it spawned. She is growing in her belief that she is a loved and valuable person.

Closely related to the conviction that "I am not loved" is the belief that "I am not lovable." The former is based upon actual experiences from which the child feels and concludes that he has been rejected by significant persons in his life. The second belief, which almost always follows the first, is the inference that the reason one is not loved by others is because some terrible defect has made one unlovable and unworthy of love. To believe "I am not lovable" is to incorporate into the self-concept the presumption that not only in the past and in the present, *but in the future as well*, I will be rejected, unwanted, and unloved by others. Often this belief comes from very real but forgotten feelings of being rejected in the distant past. These feelings and the wound of sadness they create may not be rational or "make sense;" such is the perplexing effect of memories first established during infancy. Unfortunately for many depressed persons, this "I am not lovable" element of the self-concept is built up from infancy and preserved at all costs. There is great resistance to healing this core of woundedness deep within the self.

Perhaps at this point it would be good to note that one of the primary expressions of resentment is blame. As the reader reflects on these pages concerning the effects of early childhood experiences, there may be a tendency to blame one's parents. It is important to recall, however, that depression has many causes in addition to these developmental roots. Indeed, it is hard to conceive of depression as solely based upon a mother's neglect or a traumatic experience. Because spiritual healing is *God's work in us*, it is not really essential that we dig around in our pasts for painful memories. When painful memories of past experiences do come to the surface of our consciousness, we can then invite the Lord to shine his healing light upon these areas of darkness and woundedness. Thus our remembrance of pain may become a source of grace and healing rather than a cause for resentment and blame. Understanding why we are the way we are opens the way to healing and removes much of the darkness, sorrow, and confusion which surrounds the state of depression.

The belief that "I am not lovable" is related to the guilt feelings which have their genesis in early childhood. As the infant grows and develops he becomes less and less helpless. He no longer requires the constant attention of feeding, cleansing, and holding that he did in the first months of life. Toward the end of the first year and into the second year the child must deal with several significant changes in his relationship to other persons. Weaning

may be the first of these separations from mother's primary attention, often creating with this older child a keen sense of abandonment and rejection. (Even the best mothering often cannot prevent
the sense of loss which normally occurs as the child grows up.) The
crisis in this period according to psychoanalyst Erik Erikson is
whether the young child will develop a healthy sense of himself as a
unique "little" person or whether he will be overcome by feelings
of shame and doubt as a result of becoming more independent.
Doubts and guilt feelings result from the child's irrational conclusion that the reason why he has lost mother's constant care and
attention is because of his "badness," his inability to meet
mother's expectations. This conviction that he is bad—and therefore unlovable—becomes a part of the growing self-concept. As
the child becomes older, this guilt (which is objectively unreasonable and almost entirely unconscious) causes him to develop expectations of punishment and rejection. Within this early childhood
experience of guilt, common to many of us, are the seeds of
inability to accept forgiveness from others and from God. Thus "I
am neither lovable nor forgivable" is also incorporated into the
child's self-concept together with "I am not loved."

An example of this woundedness of the self-concept is seen in
the life of Tom, whose deep seated feelings of inadequacy and
unworthiness created so much anxiety that they hampered his
ability to perform well in his college studies (*see* Chapter IV).
People described as *over*-cooperative, *over*-conscientious and self-
sacrificing are often particularly susceptible to depression. Tom's
personality fit this description. He stored unexpressed, painful
angers deep within himself, fearing any disclosure of these feelings
would result in rejection. Thus, as a growing child and adolescent
Tom felt uncertain of his parents' love, always fearful that he
would lose their love if he was unable to measure up to their high
expectations for him. He was overwhelmed by perfectionistic
feelings and, strive as he might, he could not accomplish the high
standards he set for himself; his deepest self believed "I am not

lovable.'' Tom's healing, like Janet's began with a faith-imagination prayer for inner healing and then deepened in the days and months that followed as he experienced self-acceptance and acceptance of others in his daily life.

As we have seen, events of early life play a major role in shaping feelings and ideas about one's self, about others, and about life in general. One way we make life more bearable is to forget or suppress thoughts and memories that are fearful or are painful. We do this as a matter of course, scarcely realizing the effect this suppressed material will have on our future. Thus, these deeply buried non-rational beliefs and memories continue to affect the way we cope with life. For example, the exasperating tendency to withhold forgiveness from others and oneself may be carried throughout life. Unless these firmly entrenched patterns are healed, the stage is set for an unhappy adulthood.

The memories and beliefs of the growing person are also carried over into one's relationship with God. If parents and friends are perceived as capricious and undependable in their bestowal of love, care and acceptance, then it is also likely that God will be seen in the same way. If parental and peer affection are perceived as based upon "being good" or "being perfect," then it becomes natural to believe that God's love is also dependent upon how well one strives for and attains "goodness." If a person believes he is not loved, accepted and forgiven by those persons closest to him, how can he possibly be expected to develop a deep trust in a God who loves, accepts and forgives unconditionally? A problem for many depressed people is that they can find no rational or meaningful explanation for these unrelenting feelings of sadness kindled by their depression. Wishing sadness away is of little avail. God's help *is* of avail, and that is what spiritual healing is about.

The Wound of Sadness

Throughout this book we have discussed many characteristics of depression and their physical, intellectual and emotional causes.

In this chapter we have identified sadness as a principal manifestation of depression in the spiritual life. Like the physical and psychological elements of depression, this sadness may often affect the health of the whole person (body, mind and spirit). Keeping in mind what has already been said about the "roots" of unforgiveness, we will now describe the "tree" of sadness.

Sadness is a wound deep within the spiritual self-concept. It often produces considerable suffering for the depressed person and may be viewed as a "tree that thrives in darkness." The twin roots of this tree— (1) the belief that one is unloved, with the perplexing inability to forgive (resentment), and (2) the belief that one is unlovable, with resistance to accepting forgiveness (perfectionism)—distort one's perception of the present and dims one's expectations for the future. This "tree" of darkness cannot flourish in the light which God's unconditional and healing love brings. The Lord longs to heal spiritual sadness by leading us out of darkness: he brings glad tidings to the lowly, heals the brokenhearted, proclaims liberty to captives and release to those who are prisoners (Is 61:1).

In fact, Jesus said of himself, "I am the light of the world. No follower of mine shall wander in the dark; he shall have the light of life" (Jn 8:12).

The psalmist exults in God's healing, loving presence: "You indeed, O Lord, give light to my lamp; O my God, you brighten the darkness about me" (Ps 18:28).

Throughout the remaining pages of this chapter we will refer often to the Psalms. As one reads through these "songs of God," one finds portrayed there, often in vivid intensity, every deeply human emotion. There are indeed few feelings which we experience in our daily lives which have not been described by the authors of the Psalms. The pain of abandonment, injustice, sorrow, fear, confusion, darkness, guilt, and sin are all there, prefaced almost always with a cry for help. And nearly always, as a companion prayer, are statements of trust, of hope, and of joy in a loving God who saves. We will rely on the Psalms to express the wound of sadness and its consequences in our lives, but more important yet, we include the Psalms because they contain, we believe, inspiration and power to heal.

At the beginning of this chapter we presented the story of Marie. Her wound of sadness afflicted not only her spiritual life, but her total being. She was weak and drained of energy. She was downhearted and confused. Having withdrawn from contact with her friends and family, her isolation produced great loneliness. Her sadness had so paralyzed her physically and emotionally that she did not provide for her own basic needs. She was overcome by feelings of shame and guilt, worthlessness and failure. Unable to pray, she questioned God's love for her. In Chapter VI we described the effects of depression on the spiritual life in terms of darkness. The wound of sadness with which many are afflicted is nurtured by this darkness of guilt, emptiness, and doubt. As we talked with Marie, these central elements emerged:

1) The wound of sadness is deeply related to a profound sense of *guilt* over one's imperfection. Persons who suffer from depression are so often perfectionists who set unreachable standards for themselves. Their inevitable failure to attain these standards of perfection creates a dominating sense of being burdened or weighted down. Such is emotional paralysis.

The psalmist prays: "Lord, do not punish me in your rage . . . . My guilt is overwhelming me, it is too heavy a burden . . . . Bowed down, bent double, overcome, I go mourning all the day" (Ps 38:1, 4, 6).

And then, as we find in most of the Psalms, there is a prayer of trust and willingness to accept God's saving grace: "I put my trust in you, Lord, and leave you to answer for me. Lord my God, come quickly to my help. God, my savior!" (Ps 38:15,22).

In the gospel we find Jesus' response to those who cry out for help with their burden of guilt. Jesus says to us as he did to the paralytic in Capernaum, "Courage, my child, your sins are forgiven,'' and then he healed him physically. To the crowds he said, ''Come to me, all you who labor and are overburdened, and I will give you rest. Shoulder my yoke and learn from me, for I am gentle and humble in heart, and you will find rest for your souls. Yes, my yoke is easy and my burden light'' (Mt 9:2; 11:28-30).

2) The wound of sadness also creates a gnawing *emptiness* associated with the disquieting sense that friends have become strangers and we are ''dead to love.'' The Psalmist prays, ''I cry out in the night before thee . . . . For my soul is full of troubles, and my life draws near to Sheol. I am reckoned among those who go down to the Pit; I am a man who has no strength, like one forsaken among the dead, like the slain that lie in the grave, like those whom thou dost remember no more, for they are cut off from thy hand. . . . Afflicted and close to death from my youth up, I suffer terrors; I am helpless'' (Ps 88:1, 3-5, 15).

But Jesus' promise to us is this: ''I have come that you may have *life* and have it to the full . . . . I have told you this so that my own joy may be in you, and your joy may be complete'' (Jn 10:10; 15:11).

Each one of us as a believer in Jesus is invited to share in the life and death of the Lord. Christ's life was a continual process of emptying. Paul exhorts us to imitate Jesus: ''Though he was in the form of God, he did not deem equality with God something to be grasped at. Rather, he emptied himself and took the form of a slave, being born in the likeness of men . . . he humbled himself, obediently accepting even death, death on a cross'' (Ph 2:6-8).

In everything Jesus surrendered himself to his Father: he emptied himself of his own will, plans, and claims to greatness. He opened for us the channel of grace and forgiveness. As we are emptied, channels of grace open in our lives. When we suffer in spirit from the wounds of sadness, we can either remain paralyzed in the darknes, or we can surrender ourselves, dare to let our self-image change, become trusting enough to make room for God where we ache most. As we gradually empty out our ''depressed self''—that is, the informity, imperfection, sadness and sin sustained by depression—we create a home within our spirit which can then be filled with the healing Spirit of God. By his grace and because he loves us we are able to empty ourselves so that he can fill us. Thus, we die to ourselves so that he can raise us to new life.

3) The wound of sadness thrives on the *doubt* that I am loved, which leads to resentment. To truly believe that one is not loved by others is perhaps the most wounding of all human experiences. Resentment and the feeling of being cheated follow almost naturally, although for many this resentment is disguised in depression. The Psalmist prays: ''Be gracious, O Lord, for I am in distress, and my eyes are dimmed with grief. Strong as I am, I stumble under my load of misery. There is disease in all my bones. My neighbors find me a burden, my friends shudder at me . . . . I have come to be like something lost'' (Ps 31:9-12). Then comes his prayer of abandonment to God's care: ''My days are in your hand, rescue me . . . . Save me in your love. Blessed be the Lord who performs marvels of love for me'' (Ps 31:14, 16, 21).

In a parable Jesus tells us of his love: ''Suppose a man has one hundred sheep and one of them strays; will he not leave the ninety-nine on the hillside and go in search of the stray? If he finds it, it gives him more joy than do the ninety-nine that did not stray. *It is never the will of your Father that one of these little ones should be lost* . . . . I am the good shepherd: the good shepherd is one who lays down his life for his sheep'' (Mt 18:12-14; Jn 10:11).

We are all weak in many ways. Guilt, emptiness and doubt each magnify that weakness so keenly felt by the depressed person. Time and again we fail to meet our own standards and the expectations of others. Although we strive to ''measure up'' in all that we are and do, we seldom seem to achieve the perfection which is our heart's desire. That is, after all, our human condition. We are bound to make mistakes, we are bound to sin. No matter how strong or resourceful we are, we will never be strong or resourceful enough to save ourselves. We are in need of a savior.

God, as our lifesaving God, rescues us from our sadness and brings spiritual healing. He gives strength to forgive and to accept forgiveness. Spiritual healing is truly the work of God. In some instances it appears to be God's sovereign will that individuals are instantaneously healed of their woundedness, but this does not seem to be His ordinary way. More often, the healing of inner sadness is gradual and comes with the help of others. Many will never be entirely free from sadness which makes prayer so difficult, yet God works persistently within our hearts to rescue, to heal, and to transform our resentment and perfectionism into an acceptance that is life changing. For the depressed person this process of spiritual healing or acceptance may happen as the deepest hopes for one's life are shared with a trusted friend. Those who suffer with inner sadness and find private or personal prayer a dry and unfruitful exercise are encouraged to begin communicating with a person who is able to listen and give encouragement. Often personal prayer will be blessed with a new freshness as a result.

Earlier in this book we described helplessness which is so characteristic of depression. Depressed persons almost always feel that they are helpless when it comes to taking charge of their lives. This leaves them feeling vulnerable to life's whims. Strangely enough, the spiritual healing of depression is intimately related to the willingness to accept our powerlessness. This is not the same as becoming resigned to helplessness or to a permanent state of passivity and depression. Rather, freedom from crippling wounds comes when we are able to surrender to the great power of Jesus Christ.

The New Testament, particularly the writings of the apostle Paul, teaches us that the Christian call is a call to accept the strength of God in our very weakness. Paul wrote of this to the Church at Corinth: "The God who said, 'Out of darkness the light shall shine!' is the same God who made his light shine in our hearts, to bring us the light of the knowledge of God's glory. Yet we who have this spiritual treasure are like common clay pots, to show that the supreme power belongs to God, not to us. We are often troubled, but not crushed; sometimes in doubt, but never in despair; there are many enemies but we are never without a friend; and though badly hurt at times, we are not destroyed. At all times we carry in our mortal bodies the death of Jesus, so that his life also may be seen in our bodies'' (2 Cor 4:6-10). Later in the same letter Paul described how three times he begged the Lord to heal his thorn in the flesh. The Lord's response to Paul was this: ''My grace is all you need; for my power is strongest when you are weak.'' Paul goes on to say, ''I am most happy, then, to be proud of any weakness, in order to feel the protection of Christ's power over me. I am content with weaknesses . . . for when I am weak, then I am strong'' (2 Cor 12:8-10).

What is the weakness of which scripture speaks? Reviewing what has been said above, it is something which affects our total being—body, mind, and spirit. In our bodies we suffer a variety of physical infirmities. The limitations of our minds and hearts continually keep our imperfections before us. Spiritually, our weakness is manifested by our sadness and sinfulness which are fully overcome only by the power of Jesus' death and resurrection. ''Infirm, imperfect, sad and sinful'' speaks of powerlessness. Whenever we are unable to forgive another or to accept the repentance of another we are directly confronted with our own weakness! Marie felt powerless to forgive or to be forgiven. She recognized her need to ask for God's help. We are people in need of a savior, a savior who alone is strong, perfect, joyful and holy. As we embrace weakness, often with the help of a friend, we are drawn to a deeper life of prayer and dependence upon God. We may experience God's strength in our weakness, his life in our emptiness, his love in our resentments. To embrace weakness—which paradoxically leads to wholeness—demands a humility which depends on Christ and which accepts the cross. This humility which is *Truth* calls for us to bring everything of ourselves to our understanding, compassionate Lord. To live in weakness is to live in the saving power of Jesus Christ. Like the recovering member of Alcoholics Anonymous who admits he is powerless over alcohol and must rely on a Higher Power for help, the individual who is wounded by sadness has need to acknowledge his powerlessness to help himself. As he does so, placing his trust in God and others, he discovers that "When I am weak, then I am strong."

The wound of depression in our spirit known as sadness makes it difficult to reach out to God or others for help. Our spirit imbued with sadness, we isolate ourselves. Although others may reach out to us, our first instinct is to draw away. When we are hurting so much, we paradoxically respond as though we want to keep our hurt to ourselves and to ward off the gentleness and compassion of others which might somehow shatter our hostility and guilt. As we have already emphasized, what we need more than anything else is to allow God and others to come into our sadness, for they alone with love can begin to tear down the walls which so invincibly guard our false beliefs about ourselves. This experience of being loved breaks the bondage of resentments and perfectionism. Unless we feel loved we feel unwelcome in the light of God.

Elizabeth, the depressed schoolteacher whose story is recounted in Chapter VII, told of an experience in prayer which profoundly affected her. Elizabeth set high standards for herself; she was not content unless she did well in all of her activities and relationships. This obsessive perfectionism was particularly troublesome in her spiritual life, which led to a chronic feeling of being unworthy of God's love and care. As she reflected on her secret weaknesses—her angers and resentments, her doubts and fears—she became convinced that no one, not even God, could possibly love her. One evening in church Elizabeth knelt before the Lord in prayer and began to pour out her heart to him. As she prayed in silence she imagined God speaking to her: "Elizabeth, I love you."

"Oh, no. Lord, you couldn't love me," she protested at once.

"Elizabeth, I said I love you," she heard him say it again.

"But Lord, you know the real me . . . . You can't possibly love *me*," she again protested.

And yet a third time came his word: "Elizabeth, I *do* love you!" The word of the Lord for Elizabeth was as Isaiah the prophet promises: "As the rain and the snow come down from heaven and do not return until they have watered the earth, making it blossom and bear fruit, and give seed for sowing and bread to eat, so shall the word which comes from my mouth prevail; it shall not return to me fruitless without accomplishing my purpose or succeeding in the task I gave it" (Is 55:10-11).

The thrice-repeated "I love you" was a healing word which penetrated to the depths of Elizabeth's heart. From that evening she began to recover from her feelings of worthlessness and to experience a new relationship with God in which she could confidently rest assured that she was his forgiven and much-beloved daughter.

When in the depths of sadness and powerlessness, we need *others* to speak words of healing for us. The words of God are such healing words; as the Psalmist says, "The words of the Lord are pure words, silver refined in a crucible, gold seven times purified; the voice of the Lord is power" (Ps 12:6; 29:4). We cannot easily talk ourselves out of our deepest hurts; for this we need a healer.

While Jesus is our healer par excellence, we have need for human friendships which also heal us. In fact, the Lord ministers healing to us through our friends, making them mediators of *his* friendship for us.

Friendship is healing and life-changing. Our friends help us accept ourselves as loved and lovable persons. In this way we learn "I matter to others. I am loved and lovable." As we enjoy the friendship of others we find ourselves both affirmed and challenged. Friends affirm us by loving us for who we are, but true friends also challenge and encourage us to grow into the whole persons we have the potential to become. The give and take of friendship immediately confronts the depressed person with a very real problem: accepting love and help from others. For many it is easier to assist than to be assisted. Our weaknesses are our most guarded secrets. Sometimes the same is true of our genuine needs. Thus, the transition from helping to being helped, from loving to being loved is difficult, often creating embarrassment and awkwardness. Friendship requires that we let others respond to our need.

Love, healing and acceptance flow in both directions. Friendship is healing not only because of acceptance we *receive* from others, but also because of what we *give* of ourselves to others. How necessary it is to be loved! How equally necessary it is to give love! From all that depressed people have experienced and endured, what treasures of compassion and wisdom they have to share with others! Among friends the roles of "helper" and "being helped" are intertwined continually in an understanding exchange which is enriching and healing for both persons. It is in speaking the words of our hearts to another and in our attentiveness both to others in conversation and to God in prayer, that the heavy weight of our unforgiving and perfectionistic nature is no longer borne alone. In relationships such as these there is shared peace, inner joy, and a growing ability to love and to be loved. Healed and healing persons accept themselves both as persons who need help and as persons who help others. Swiss theologian Paul Tillich said that "Faith is the courage to accept acceptance." This indeed is our challenge: to accept the acceptance of our friends and our Lord, and for this we need trusting faith.

Jesus the compassionate Lord and merciful savior is our healer. Jesus brings light into the darkness of sadness: "I, the light, have come into the world so that whoever believes in me need not stay in the dark anymore" (Jn 12:46). Jesus loves us though we believe ourselves unlovable. He accepts and forgives us though we feel and believe ourselves unacceptable and unforgivable. More primary than the love of mother or father, brother or sister or closest of friends, is the love which God has for us. The love of God is both priceless and costless. His grace-filled healing love does not depend on our goodness, worthiness, or personal holiness. It is not a prize we earn by living up to his expectations. The love which God has for us is totally unconditional: ''When we were still powerless, Christ died for us . . . . It is precisely in this that God proves his love for us: that while we were yet sinners, Christ died for us'' (Rm 5:6, 8). God loves us as we are. He does not require of us great achievements, but asks instead for our total selves so that he can make us whole and well and peaceful through the healing power of his loving Spirit. As persons who have been deeply and often secretly wounded by the conviction that we are unloved and unlovable, perhaps the most significant step we can take toward spiritual healing is to open our minds, hearts, and spirits to this unfathomable and healing love of God. The pages of this book are filled with true stories from the lives of men and women who have taken this step in their journey. All of these people have, in some individual way, wondered how God could ever help them, and then by the power of his grace invited God to come and visit them, to bring help. And, as we have seen, each person's journey is different; there is no one single way in which God restores health and wholeness.

EPILOGUE

May the God of our Lord Jesus Christ, the Father of glory, grant you a spirit of wisdom and insight to know him clearly. May he enlighten your innermost vision that you may know the great hope to which he has called you, the wealth of his glorious heritage to be distributed among the members of the church, and the immeasurable scope of his power in us who believe (Ep 1:17-19a).

We journey mile by mile and day by day as we encounter life. As we travel the path which leads us from mountain peaks to fertile valleys to arid deserts, we come to know that our growth and healing requires time and patience. We cannot experience the whole of our lives in any one moment, nor can we anticipate in any exact way what our future holds. However, if we only judge our days and miles ahead by days gone by and by distances already traveled, our sights are not set on our inheritance in Christ Jesus. As Paul writes to the Ephesians, God enlightens our innermost vision and this awakens hope. God does this not only by inspiration but also by giving us others. The ideas of this book and the people about whom it is written may bring understanding and hope when your journey leads you through depression or into darkness.

As you reflect about the many ways by which depression may manifest itself in one's journey, you immediately realize that each person's struggle with this disorder is deeply personal and unique. True, there are identifying signs by which professionals diagnose and treat depression. As we have seen, however, these physical, mental and spiritual signs emerge during our life in different ways at different times. Similarly, some avenues of treatment and healing may be more effective than others, depending on the nature and expression of depression. What might be recommended and successful for one person may be of little help to another. Some forms of treatment may prove useful as temporary remedies while others should become a way of life. It is the authors' hope that you gain a better understanding of how depression may manifest itself in your own and others' lives. Perhaps then it will be easier to conquer those aspects of this disorder which can be cured and to accept those which cannot be changed. The healing strength of the Lord is present not only when we conquer but also when we accept.

Wellsprings of hope and healing are found in the lives of many who have and do journey by night. We complete this book with the written accounts of two such travelers. Judith is a wife and mother of five children. She writes of her ongoing painful passage from her lonely prison of perfectionism and depression to the freedom which comes when we let others accept us as we truly are. Robert is a rancher and regional director of 4-H youth programs. In his account he emphasizes how heavy the burden of disguise can be on one's journey through life, and tells how for him the cross of depression is made lighter through acceptance.

JUDITH: I FACE THE WORLD

How does one actually begin to tell about feelings as difficult as depression and the faith crisis that can accompany it? As a young child I had polio. I was only seven and maybe that's why I remember only bits and pieces. I remember nothing of the years before I became ill. Quite naturally, I recall certain episodes that occurred during the initial months of my illness. What I remember most is pain. At the same time I began to see that I had to handle myself and my problems in a perfect, cheerful manner to receive the praise and encouragement I wanted and needed from my doctors and family. Such is the way a child views her situation. I worked very hard at being the perfect patient and I worked just as hard at being the perfect child of God.

I did not tell how I really felt about all that was happening to me. I didn't talk about fear, the embarrassment of the crutches, brace and ugly shriveled leg, the shame of the awful orthopedic shoes that attached to the brace, the horrors of being so different from the other children when I finally was able to go back to a regular school, the anger, the nightmare of trying to look happy as I stood by watching the others play. I was determined not to let anyone know how terrifying and painful all of this was for me. I had few friends during those years; I felt I was a freak. I hated the real me I kept hidden because I believed that the "inside me" who wanted to cry, rage, complain, was not acceptable—was bad. Thus, the stage was being set in my childhood for a deep, painful depression later in life.

People often commented about my cheerful nature and how I never seemed to have difficulty handling the various crises (surgeries, medical procedures, therapy, etc.) that continually came along and had to be faced without a falter. I married and had five children. During those years I had ongoing problems with my legs which resulted in a series of minor and major surgeries. Usually another surgery was necessary after another child was born. I prayed and I tried to offer up my fears about what was obviously happening to me just as I had been taught to do all of my life. And I pushed myself harder to be the perfect wife and mother and Christian. My time was filled with the activities of a housewife and any that was left over was devoted to church work. I taught religion classes, helped start and run a FISH (emergency help) organization, and was deeply involved in the Cursillo movement. I was giving everything I had; I was still striving to be that perfect person. Then the bottom fell out.

I began to have serious difficulties with my legs and went back to the hospital for more surgery on what had been considered my "good leg." This surgery, although far from my first, was more than I could handle emotionally. I was losing the use of the leg I had depended on for standing and walking. I was absolutely terrified. It was like a painful step back into the past. Years of struggle, pain and suffering had gone into getting myself up on my feet. Now I was losing that ground I had fought so hard to attain. I also knew that falling back was not allowed, but I could not express my fears or ask for the help and support I needed. I pretended to be strong as I listened to the platitudes of my religious friends: "Put it in the hands of the Lord." "What a wonderful opportunity to offer up another period of suffering." "Let me tell you about my friend who just lost her husband—that's *real* suffering." "God loves you and that's all you need to know to handle any problem." "I am saying prayers of thanksgiving for your complete recovery." (This before the surgery and with no knowledge that there could ever be complete recovery.) "God says you should pray for a complete healing and if you pray hard enough, you will be running and dancing after the operation." (This to someone who had never been able to run or really dance.) "God loves you so much because you suffer so much." (I cannot understand that kind of love.)

I could not tolerate or believe what I was hearing from my religious friends. They made me angry. This raised all kinds of guilt feelings. I was ashamed that I could not accept all their religious advice, and I judged myself a failure. I had come to the point that I could not listen to "easy" answers about my life. In fact, I could no longer even turn to God for help. Alone and lost, I knew that I had failed God and, yes, He had failed me. I could not pray. There were no beautiful words or thoughts left in me. I was past the point of pretending within myself. I was also past the point of anger at God. Before, I had felt rejected by Him because I had received nothing in return for my prayers. There had been no comfort, no answers, no strength, no understanding, no relief from pain, no peace, and, most of all, no hope. Now I know that I had failed Him. I was not a perfect child of God.

I communicated with no one about the depth of my despair and fear. Thus I did not receive the understanding and help I needed. I withdrew into myself and during that time I experienced what I consider to be the depths of depression. I wanted to die and considered various methods of taking my life. With the shower running full force so that the children wouldn't hear, I would lock myself in the bathroom and cry uncontrollably. My emotional pain was so intense that I could not stand it. Physical pain actually became a welcome distraction, and I found myself striking my painful legs in fury and frustration.

My reactions to offers of help were almost always negative. Admitting my need for help would be an acknowledgement of my weakness and the occasion for more platitudes that so often accompanied those offers. It didn't take very long for most of the people I knew to disappear. "She's so hard to help. I don't know what to do or say. What's wrong with her? After all, she's been through operations before." I know they had good reason to be confused! I was so confused about myself that they couldn't be expected to understand what I hadn't worked out and therefore couldn't and wouldn't communicate.

But there were a few who stood by me, and I thank God for them today. They didn't require all kinds of explanations; they just reacted to the hurting that they saw. They proved their caring and concern by their constant presence. They took the time to be near me when I felt like no one could want to associate with me. I believe that the first steps back from the depths of my depression depended on those human relationships. Without realizing it, these people began to heal the wounds of rejection I felt as a crippled child. Before I could even begin to search for answers about my relationship with God, I had to trust enough to build a deep, true relationship with these close friends. For me, the healing in my relationship with God came second.

The healing of my emotional wounds could begin only when I was finally able to open up to someone and to admit all the real feelings that I was having and had had throughout my life. How difficult this is when you believe that you are unlovable if you are anything other than courageous and undoubting. Haltingly, I was able to start admitting my deepest fears to my husband, and I know now that I could do this only because he stood by me and assured me even when he didn't understand me at all. He had continued to express his care and fidelity even when I had shut him out and actually rejected his gestures of love and concern. He had not given advice and he had not criticized. He had not tried to alter my behavior or reactions by making me feel guilty about anything. He did not judge; he simply tried to understand how he might help. He did not want to hear the things I needed to say! But someone had to love me enough to let me speak my fears and to deal with them honestly. It took months for all of the hurts, frustration, self-doubt, anger, and rejection to come out. It took time for him to learn how to listen. Listening is a difficult and true Christian art which so few of us learn or practice well. It was very hard for him to share my suffering in this way. But he allowed me to say that I did not have lovely ''religious'' feelings about my suffering.

For me the development of a new relationship with God depended upon assurance from someone who knew me well that I was really lovable as a complete person, faults and weaknesses included. Gradually I began to reconsider my conclusions about God. I realized that my hidden self had always been known to God, even though I had not shown my negative side willingly and openly to Him. When depression dissolved my mask of ''goodness,'' prayer as I had known it was no longer possible; I tried to hide myself from God because I believed that by admitting my weakness I had failed Him. Acceptance from my husband and friends was the key which enabled me to willingly and openly approach God again. With the mask off I could communicate with a degree of honesty I had never been capable of before, and I found that I had not grown as far away from Him as I had thought! He could see all that there was to see—all that I had spent years trying to hide and cover up—and He still loved me.

Prayer has taken on new meaning. I now pray by sharing my feelings and suffering with God. Sometimes that is all that is humanly possible. I have learned that prayer does not have to be expressed through words or even thoughts: prayer is just being present to God. I am sure that when I pray this way what I offer is honest communication with Him. There are other times when the security of familiar rote prayers, like the Lord's Prayer, is a wonderful source of comfort. Who could really put a limit on the ways we communicate with God? How can anyone who honestly tries to pray fail? How sad it is that people judge their own prayer or the prayer of others as unworthy.

The process of coming out of depression took a long time. There were times of great progress and times of regression. During that period of four years I went into the hospital five times and underwent four major surgeries, although these procedures failed to help in my case. Step by step I found the courage to face the reality of my life. I drew strength from the unconditional love of those close to me, and I began to be myself. It is a new type of life. The experience of acute depression that I have gone through has changed me as a person and it has changed my faith. In so many ways I feel like I have just begun to live. I am no longer so influenced by unreasonable expectations of perfection. I have shed much guilt and am learning to live with the real person who is me. I am letting myself BE. I am beginning to let this simple but profound concept permeate my relationship with God. I am trying to let God BE.

I have been trying to describe the feelings associated with severe depression, and it is very difficult. It goes deeper than words can express. Despair, hopelessness, anguish, fury, loneliness, coldness, darkness—even when put together these do not tell it all. Maybe sever-depression would be a better expression. It implies the breaking off of contact with God, loved ones, friends, and even reality. But with the support of loved ones who allow the inner me to be expressed, I face the world.

Judith's story once again alerts us to the powerful emotional and spiritual dimensions of our life. Sometimes one becomes so concerned with an illness, a handicap or even work that emotional and spiritual development is postponed or neglected. Judith tells how difficult it was to welcome the help of family, friends and God especially when weak like this and facing depression. Yet, the *presence* of others gave her strength. The acceptance of help is for many depressed people the key to their successful struggle toward recovery. Family and friends of the ill or depressed are reminded by Judith's story to look beyond surface expressions of human suffering to the person Judith terms the "inner me." As we have seen, caring for the "inner me" of another calls for heroic patience especially during depression. Finally, no one should bear the blame that this struggle to help and be helped is so painful or sometimes fails. Such blame quickly kindles or rekindles resentments and spiritual sadness. This puts us at a distance from those closest to us, including our inner selves.

In the isolation of depression we may wonder if we are remembered by anyone, even God. Perhaps these others do sense something of our outward lives, our problems, our accomplishments, but can they indeed be close to us in a deeper way? During trials we may have a heightened sense of (and need for) the fidelity of others. Judith sensed deeply the efforts of her husband, friends and God to remain near her even when her depression stripped her of the ability to communicate. Their patient, silent fidelity proved to be a healing force for her. It helped Judith realize the truth that our presence never fades from the hearts of those who love us and especially never from the heart of God.

ROBERT: TEARS BEHIND CLOSED DOORS

For a long time I thought nearly everyone dealt with severe levels of depression. I presumed it was a part of everyone's life and often wondered why it was so hard for me to accept and overcome. As long as my memory records, I have felt these feelings of hopelessness, sadness, almost utter despair. Many times it was difficult to find the strength to survive.

On the outside folks would say "Robert has it all together," and yet on the inside I wasn't sure I could even survive the moment. My depression cannot easily be detected by casual observation. It takes a rather close look inside those well-maintained walls to truly know how deep depression can cut.

I don't profess to understand its origin. However, I do offer my testimonial to its pain and agony: the feeling that you can no longer live through it, that you aren't in the right space of time or place, the terrible aloneness believing that only you are afflicted, the conviction that nothing you say, do, or think will lessen the pain because what you have tried before has not worked. You learn to quit looking for biological causes, cognitive roots, outside forces or passing contributors and generally learn to approach acceptance.

This feeling I call depression does not hold the same intensity at all times. There are times—even days or weeks—that it seems to lift altogether. You might even feel you'll be okay, and then for reasons I've never been able to isolate, zap! it returns.

When depression hits at its hardest I find it very difficult to perform my normal duties in the usual fashion. I often slip behind closed doors and let it flow out through tears; sometimes it streams from hand to pen; other times sleeping it away helps; even other times I fantasize that it will soon end through some externally inflicted death.

I've lived with depression for a long time now and have matured with this fact in many ways. One key concept I've learned through the help of others is acceptance, and some even advocate thanksgiving. Depression, if it showed, might be similar to being paralyzed. People can spend all their time and energy trying to change it; but peace normally will not occur until acceptance begins. To recognize it as real has been another important concept to learn in the living-with-it process. With this basic premise and a strong underlying faith, this cross takes its place in a bigger scheme and allows for even greater acceptance. Less energy is spent on running away.

When depression deepens, I now accept it and recognize it as such. I've found that vigorous physical exercise is important at this time. Being close to a friend seems to help. Reaching out to help others is also beneficial. My new philosophy is Stay Busy; Do not ignore but accept depression; Live with it, do not die because of it. Working with open eyes, open hearts and our hands joined, we will learn to understand and to accept.

Unlike Judith, Robert has shared his experiences of depression apart from circumstances of his life. Do not let Judith's powerful story divert your attention from the inner reality of depression which Robert communicates. This depression in his journey can be encountered by any one of us in our journeys. Robert does not search for the reasons of his depression; rather he continues to find thanksgiving in his heart for the cross he bears. Should his burden become heavier in the future, Robert intends to reach out for additional help. For now, and hopefully for the rest of his life, the healing grace of God prompts him to admit his depression, to attend to his physical-mental-spiritual needs, and to allow friends to bring him strength.

In closing, our prayer and wish for you so reflects the words of Paul to the Romans (8:38-39).

> That no powers of depression:
> > Not the darkness of guilt, emptiness and doubt,
> > Not the helplessness of distortion, negative thinking, and withdrawal,
> > Not the weakness and pain of body,
> > Not crippling memories or false expectations,
> > Not the failure of others to listen and to understand,
> > Not the compulsion of work or service,
> > Not any of the world's problems,
> Can keep you from a life of wholeness.

That is, *nothing* in your journey as it is or in your journey as it shall be can separate you from the love of God made visible in Christ Jesus our Lord.